"Every writer gets lost from time to time on the creative journey, and when that happens, it's nice to encounter a friendly and helpful companion like *Seven Steps on the Writer's Path*. Nancy Pickard and Lynn Lott light the path and guide us out of the darkness one step at a time."

—ROB MACGREGOR
Edgar Award–winning author of *Prophecy Rock*

"This book made me want to walk straight to the computer and start writing."

—ELAINE VIETS
Author of *Shop Till You Drop: A Dead-End Job Mystery*

"*Seven Steps on the Writer's Path* is a must-read, must-absorb, must-follow for anyone who has ever even dreamed of becoming a writer. Nancy Pickard and Lynn Lott brilliantly define the joys and jolts all of us encounter on the tortuous road to publication and beyond, along with excellent practical tips for how to stay the daunting, difficult course and make those writing dreams a reality."

—JUDITH KELMAN
Author of *Every Step You Take*

"*Seven Steps* offers much good advice, both practical and motivational, that's been time- and career-tested. This would be a pleasing companion as you embark on a book project in any genre."

—SUSAN K. PERRY
Author of *Writing in Flow: Keys to Enhanced Creativity*

"With this enlightening book for writers, we find two authors who not only understand the truth about the writer's life, but also communicate it with flat out honesty, a dose of impishness, and always an abundance of heart."

—GAIL PROVOST STOCKWELL
Cofounder, Write It/Sell It Seminars and
Workshops, and Writers Retreat Workshop

Lynn Lott

Chores Without Wars (with Riki Intner)
Do-It-Yourself Therapy: How to Think, Feel,
and Act Like a New Person in Just 8 Weeks
(with Riki Intner and Barbara Mendenhall)
Teaching Parenting the Positive Discipline Way Manual
(with Jane Nelsen)
Together and Liking It (with Dru West)
To Know Me Is to Love Me: Steps for Raising Self-Esteem
(with Marilyn Matulich Kentz and Dru West)
Positive Discipline A–Z (with Jane Nelsen and H. Stephen Glenn)
Positive Discipline in the Classroom
(with Jane Nelsen and H. Stephen Glenn)
Positive Discipline in the Classroom:
A Teacher's Guide Manual (with Jane Nelsen)
Positive Discipline for Parenting in Recovery
(with Jane Nelsen and Riki Intner)
Positive Discipline for Teenagers (with Jane Nelsen)

Nancy Pickard

The Truth Hurts
Storm Warnings
Ring of Truth
The Whole Truth
Speak No Evil
Twilight
Generous Death
Say No to Murder
Bum Steer
I.O.U.
No Body
Confession
But I Wouldn't Want to Die There
Dead Crazy
Marriage Is Murder

Seven Steps on the Writer's Path

The Journey from Frustration to Fulfillment

Lynn Lott
and *Nancy Pickard*

Ballantine Books • New York

A Ballantine Book
Published by The Random House Publishing Group

Copyright © 2003 by Nancy Pickard and Lynn Lott

Grateful acknowledgement is made to the following:
Richard Keith for permission to reprint his poem. Copyright © 2003 by Richard Keith.
Lynn Lott for permission to reprint an illustration from TO KNOW ME IS TO LOVE ME.

www.ballantinebooks.com

Library of Congress Control Number: 2003098272

ISBN 0-345-45110-4

Book designed by BTDnyc

Manufactured in the United States of America

First Hardcover Edition: August 2003
First Trade Paperback Edition: June 2004

10 9 8 7 6 5 4 3 2 1

Lynn dedicates this book to Hal with love.
"The Universe sent me someone to walk the path who inspires me, comforts me, helps me, challenges me, and loves me."

Nancy dedicates this book to her mother,
Mary Wolfe, with love and gratitude.
*"Without a mother who reads, I'd never
have become a daughter who writes."*

*Let no one be deluded that a knowledge of the path
can substitute for putting one foot in front of the other.*
—Mary Caroline Richards

Contents

· ·

Preface

How This Book Was Born

• •

A few years ago, mystery writer Nancy Pickard and psychologist and self-help author Lynn Lott were both asked to be presenters at the Bare Bones Writers Retreat put on by the San Diego Chapter of Sisters in Crime. By "bare bones," the conference organizers were referring to the accommodations at an old summer camp in the mountains and not, they no doubt hoped, to the workshop material to be given by their speakers. The problem was, however, that although Lynn, in California, knew what she would talk about to the writers there, Nancy, in Kansas, was feeling down to the bare bones herself.

Having by that time been a professional writer for more than thirty years, and having spoken to thousands of people about writing, Nancy found that she was sick of hearing herself say the same old things: where did she get her ideas, did she plot out her story first, did she work on a computer, and so on and so forth. She wondered if there might be something deeper, a larger perspective, she might contribute to the existing knowledge of the writing life.

What emerged from her musings was unexpected—a form, a structure, a pattern.

As she looked back over her own career and that of her many writer friends, she saw herself and most of them struggling through stages of unhappiness, of wanting, of commitment, of wavering, of letting go, of immersion, and of fulfillment. It looked very much like a path to her, and it felt true, the way only actual lived experience does feel true. And so she put together a workshop, "The Seven Steps on the Writer's Path."

At the conference, in a cold, dirty, cavernous room, she lined up seven chairs at the front and placed a different sign, one for each of the steps, on each chair. After explaining a bit about the steps, she asked for volunteers to fill the chairs according to which step they believed they were on at the time. All seven chairs filled up quickly, so that now seven brave strangers were gazing out at the audience, which included best-selling mystery writer Sue Grafton. Nancy asked people to tell in turn what it was like for them to be on their step, and then she opened up the discussion to the other writers there. One person realized she was sitting in the "wrong" chair, and another person hurried up to take her place. The writers in the room couldn't seem to participate fast enough. Sue Grafton volunteered her feelings about the importance of the third step, Commitment. Words tumbled out from all over the room; deep feelings emerged; there was shared laughter, some tears, fear, hope, and inspiration. The steps seemed to come alive, and they felt as authentic as Nancy believed them to be.

Lynn Lott was seated in the audience, taking notes as fast as she could and thinking that she'd love to try out the material in one of the retreats she put on for clients in her therapy practice. After the workshop, she approached Nancy and asked her permission, which Nancy gladly gave.

Later, Lynn wrote to Nancy, "I transformed your 'writer's path' into a path for mere mortals and called it their personal growth and change path. I asked them to focus on their dreams and wishes or on an accomplishment that was important to them. I suggested they could use your seven steps on the writer's path to learn more about their personal journeys. In attendance were artists, lawyers, coaches, teachers, hairdressers, personal fitness trainers, and homemakers. They loved it, and it helped frame the entire weekend with a common language."

Nancy wrote back, suggesting they do a book together, and that's how it all began.

After that, and over the next two years, they worked in person and by E-mail. They wrote together in Florida and in California. Lynn wrote first drafts, and Nancy ripped them to shreds; Nancy wrote first drafts, and Lynn took scissors to them. Meanwhile, Lynn continued to use the steps with her therapy clients, testing the material out "in the field," in real life. Some of her clients are artists of one sort or another, but that doesn't seem to matter in regard to the applicability of the steps. She has found in her practice that the steps apply to everyone, not just to writers or to people who think of themselves as creative.

Nancy and Lynn interviewed dozens of writers at all stages of careers, ranging from those who only daydream about writing to actual beginners, apprentices, and masters. They scoured literature looking for what famous dead writers had to say about their creative process. You'll find many of them quoted in this book, along with the living ones, because what they all had to say about the writing life is instructive and entertaining.

Gradually, as the coauthors wrote and rewrote, argued and cogitated, they seemed to mutate into one voice/one brain that felt to them like having a third writer in the room. It is that "third writer" who wrote this book, but it is Nancy and Lynn who hope with all their hearts that you, too, can identify with these steps and that this book will help you navigate your own writing life with skill, pleasure, and daring.

The Trailhead
Starting Out

••

*I had not thought of myself as geography, as invisible, internal
lines I could chart, but the more I searched, the more things
connected, until the rivers and the memories became a story,
and also, perhaps a map.*

—Paul Zalis, *Who Is the River*

*Standing on a high point, I can look off in every direction over
a vast landscape. Dark shadows are settling in the valleys and
gulches and the heights are made higher and the depths deeper
by the glamour and witchery of light and shade.*
. . . [T]he country is marked "Unexplored."

—John Wesley Powell, *Down the Colorado*

Writing is a path as full of darkness as it is of light, and
so the way ahead is hard to see. There are so many omi-
nous shadows, unpredictable gusts of wind, unexpected,
blinding shafts of sunlight. It's easy to get lost, to trip over our own
hidden roots, or plunge unaware into unexplored caverns in our psyche. As writers, we hardly ever know exactly where we're going. The
only thing that most of us know how to do is to keep putting one foot
after the other in the darkness and trust that eventually we'll get
there.

Like every other writer we know, we have been lost on the writing
path more times than there are rocks in the dirt. There have been
times when we've frantically fumbled for a light when the way got

dark. At other times, we've allowed the light to dazzle and deceive us. But we've kept going, step by fumbling, bleeding step, because that's what writers do when they don't know what else to do—they just keep putting pen to paper, until they find their way out again.

If that sounds melodramatic, it's because the writing path is a bit over the top. Anyone who walks it finds that out through hard experience. Terror! Laughter! Tears! Jeers! It's an adventure story, a romance, a drama, a situation comedy, a tragedy, and a farce. This can be a hard place for the fainthearted or the emotionally cautious to spend any time. On the other hand, this path is also beautiful and is just as likely to bring you peace of mind as it is to dismay you. We know people who would give their souls to walk it and many others who claim to have found their souls upon it.

When we first began to write, there was no book to tell us, "You are here on the writer's path." We didn't even know there was a path, much less a map to it. Most writers don't, which makes them all the braver for stumbling on through the underbrush without even a trail to follow. Maybe you've been floundering along as we have. Maybe you're an experienced writer who's having a midcareer crisis. Or maybe you've never written very much, but you cherish a secret dream to be a writer. Perhaps you're writing but not getting published, and you feel awful about that. Or maybe you would just like to have some perspective on where you've been and where you're going.

The act of writing is almost by definition a loss of perspective. When we're really deep into our writing, we're like those drops in the ocean that say in puzzled tones, "Where am I going? How will I get there? And what's

Be careful going in search of adventure—it's ridiculously easy to find.
—William Least Heat-Moon

Traveling is like falling in love: the world is made new.
—Jan Myrdal

this water stuff I keep hearing about?" As writers, we can get so isolated and so caught up in our passion for writing that we can hardly tell up from down or gauge distances or see the horizon. Without perspective on what we're doing, we can feel confused and alone. We can so easily forget that we're surrounded by other writers and that all of us are being carried along by the same great currents of language and desire.

Would it help to know that you are probably not lost at all but merely stalled on a real step along a real path? Would it help to learn about some ways to get you moving forward again? With this book, this map to the writer's life, we hope to help you do just that. We will lay out the path for you and teach you how to pinpoint your location on it. We trust that when you know where you are and what you're doing there, you will feel encouraged and relieved, and that will release your creative energy. At the very least, we have hopes that you will take comfort and solace from the company of other writers who know exactly how you feel, as nobody else in the world can really know.

At first glance, it wouldn't seem as if there could be one path for everybody. In creative endeavors, how could there be just one direction to go? In fact, the writer's path can look deceptively different for each of us. There are writers who feel irresistibly called to this path. For others, it looks like a detour on their way to other things. For some, it is a spiritual path, while others approach it for material reasons or to play with it. Only for a lucky few does it feel as straightforward as a sidewalk. And yet there is an underlying process we all go through, a series of steps that are common to all of us.

Those steps form a map to the creative process.

What is traveling? Changing your place? By no means! Traveling is changing your opinions and your prejudices.

—Anatole France

The best preparation for work is not thinking about work, talking about work, or studying for work: it is work.

—William Weld

Not every writer who reads this book will agree with the terminology we've chosen or with the route we've mapped out. We all have to be true to our own experience of these things. But the authors have found so much agreement about these steps when we interviewed other writers that we hope you will consider their relevance to your own way of thinking about and experiencing creativity.

The Ebb and Flow of Creativity

A basic premise of this book is that going forward into feeling is the way out of being stuck anywhere along this path. Just as waves in the ocean surge all the way forward without hesitation, so are writers best served by surging all the way forward onto each of these steps in order to build up sufficient momentum to carry them further along. Feeling this path deeply is important; feeling each step fully is important and is also, as we have discovered, a cure for writer's block.

It is a fact of nature that when things reach their extreme—like waves in the ocean—they naturally begin to turn around in the other direction. They have to be allowed to reach their full extent, or they will simply peter out, like a wave that dies on the shore. When that happens in writing, we're like an archer who pulls his arrow only partway back before trying to shoot it. Writers need the momentum of the ocean of creativity within us; we need enough energy to fly as straight and true as an arrow released from a taut bow. Walking the writer's path halfheartedly won't do that; living and feeling it fully will.

Which is not to say it's always easy.

Life is a great big canvas and you should throw all the paint on it you can.
—Danny Kaye

Go the extra mile. It's never crowded.
—*Executive Speechwriter Newsletter*

Some of the steps along the writer's path are hard to face; some are a joy.

Step one is Unhappiness, and who wants to endure that? Fortunately, it's often experienced only as a creative itch, which is easier to take. Wherever along the continuum of Unhappiness we happen to fall on any given day of writing, these feelings must be acknowledged and felt if they are going to propel us powerfully on to the next step. In fact, the key words for doing step one are *feel* and *reveal*, which you will learn more about in the "Unhappiness" chapter.

Step two, Wanting, is no less challenging for some writers to endure if they've grown up being convinced that it's not nice to want things or if they think they aren't evolved if they feel desire. They're going to have to let themselves feel it deeply if they ever hope to get much further along before running out of steam. The key words for accomplishing this step are *focus* on our desires and *collect* whatever we need to make them happen.

Commitment, step three, comes more easily to some writers than to others, as is true of any of the steps. Some just seem to have a natural talent for accomplishing the key elements of this step, which are *give attention* to what we want most, *decide* to go after it, and then *set it in motion*. If that doesn't come easily to you, then learning what's required may help you become a more committed writer.

Step four, Wavering, is a tough one, because it comes as such a shock after the determination of Commitment. Here, writers have to *face fears* and *align core values* in order to be able to get to the point of . . .

Letting Go, which is step five. Here, you'll feel the

The writing of a play is the most enjoyable part of it. It's also the most frightening part because you walk into a forest without a knife, a compass.
—Neil Simon

If you wait, all that happens is that you get older.
—Larry McMurtry

The work will teach you how to do it.
—Estonian proverb

sweet release of *relief* and *crossing over* to the actual work you have longed to do.

Step six is Immersion. This is the work, at last. The key words here are *resolve*, which is something different from commitment, and *preoccupied*, that delicious state of being in the writer's trance.

Fulfillment, step seven, is not synonymous with "being published." This step isn't about that—at least, not necessarily. It's about *endings* and *beginnings* and about *celebration*, the key words to doing this step so well that it cycles us right back around to the beginning of the writer's path once more.

This path is not a loop, however—at least, not if you're continuing to grow as a writer. It's more like a spiral, winding around and around, over and over, never repeating itself, and yet always running along a familiar track as it ascends. It carries its own momentum, but only so long as the writer fills up on the fuel of each step to get her along to the next one.

There are seven steps and many writers, and one size does not fit all. Each of us will travel this path in our own unique way; no two experiences of it will be identical. And yet we do share certain important things in common. We're here because we love writing, or we're curious about it, we want to write, or we want to write better, or we want to be more successful in our writing, whatever *successful* means to each of us. And surely it's true that we'd all like to live full, rich, creative lives, fulfilling our best potentials, if we possibly can. Our separate journeys along this path may look quite different one from the other in their particulars, but at the heart of them is a process that we share at a fundamental and honest level, and that is the writer's path. We believe that by acknowledging that process, by understanding

You take your material where you find it, which is in your life, at the intersection at past and present. The memory-traffic feeds into a rotary up in your head, where it goes in circles for awhile, then pretty soon imagination flows in and the traffic merges and shoots off down a thousand different streets. As a writer, all you can do is pick a street and go for a ride.

—Tim O'Brien

these steps, and by living them consciously, we can help ourselves and we will help one another.

Are you ready to start down the path or to locate yourself upon it? You're among friends now, so let's go. Pull on your hiking boots, keep this book as your map, fill up the thermos with hot coffee, stuff a notebook and a pencil in your backpack, and follow us.

Unhappiness

Step One on the Writer's Path

∙∙

Who would want to live with a novelist? A man underfoot in the house all day? A man, moreover, subject to solitary funks and strange elations. If I were a woman, I'd prefer a traveling salesman.

—Walker Percy

The writer's only responsibility is to his art. He will be completely ruthless if he is a good one. He has a dream. It anguishes him so much he must get rid of it. He has no peace until then. Everything goes by the board: honor, pride, decency, security, happiness, all, to get the book written.

—William Faulkner

Q: How do you feel before you know what it is you're going to write next?
A: Lonesome.

—Eva McCall

Toddlers earn the nickname "terrible twos" because they're bursting with the anxiety and helplessness of having feelings that they can't get anybody around them to understand. They could explode with the frustration of not being able to say what they want and to explain what they're feeling. They don't even have the right words in their heads yet—it's all emotion and frustration.

That's also an accurate description of writers in step one.

This initial state of anxiety and frustration is one of the hardest things about being a writer, partly because we so often go through it alone. The solitary life of a writer can be a joy, especially for the more introverted among our tribe, but there's not much joy to be had if we're here on this step by ourselves. And if we aren't alone, there's not much joy for the people around us, either.

As if it's not humbling enough to admit that writers have something in common with two-year-olds, it is also true that writers are a lot like werewolves and timber rattlers. We get that itchy feeling under our skin before the change. Psychiatrist Carl G. Jung called this irritable, anxious, restless condition the "precreative state." We call it unhappiness. The only cure for it is to write, although not immediately. Just as it takes a while for a toddler to learn to talk and for a rattler to shake out of its old skin, so it can take writers a while to work through this step. The trick is to be able to live through it and then to emerge on the other side with both our sanity and our creativity intact, and that is easier said than done, as any longtime writer—or the spouse of a writer—can attest.

Unhappiness by Any Other Name

Call this first step in the creative process what you will, according to your own experience of it. Name it the "creative urge," if you like. Call it an "itch" or "creative tension" or "restlessness" or "discontent." Regardless of what label any of us gives this step, it's a common state and the first step for all of us.

Unhappiness, to one degree or another, is where all creativity begins.

The defense force inside of us wants us to be cautious, to stay away from anything as intense as a new kind of action. Its job is to protect us, and it categorically avoids anything resembling danger. But it's often wrong.

—Barbara Sher

Creativity means, by definition, change. If we were perpetually content with our status quo, we'd never change, and there would never be any need for creativity. Fortunately, we human beings are rarely content with the status quo, and so the need to be creative arises naturally in us. It is the various versions of unhappiness that alert us to when the creative process is about to begin again.

If you're starting to feel that itch, you're moving into step one.

Some writers told us that they never feel this first step as actual unhappiness but rather as a low-level frustration or restlessness. They say it is almost pleasurable to them, rather like the buildup of sexual tension. They know what it means and what's coming down the line, and they welcome it.

The reason we insist on calling it "unhappiness" is that what they call "tension" can very quickly turn into discomfort and then into misery if left unattended. When writers or would-be writers get stuck in this step, *unhappiness* is hardly a strong enough word to describe what they are going through. They would dearly love to be able to call it "creative tension," because that's the sort of thing you can release, like steam from a kettle. Unhappiness, further down the continuum, is a harder nut to crack.

We have found that there are two secrets to doing this step well and keeping it from turning into long-running misery. We will investigate those secrets in depth in this chapter. Briefly, for now, the first of those is *feeling it* as deeply and honestly as you can, as soon as you can, and for as long as it takes to let that tension burst forth into creativity. The second secret is *revealing it* as soon as you recognize it, which means being honest with yourself and other people.

This is no easy task, but then there's probably no other step along this path that so dramatically separates the self-aware from the self-deceiving. And that's also the beauty of it, because good writers are honest, starting with themselves. If there is any step that will keep you honest, this is the one.

Let Us Now Praise Unhappiness

Writers are supposed to be among the luckiest people on earth. Doesn't practically everybody you know say they wish they could be a writer? How can a writer be unhappy? How dare a writer be unhappy?

Oh, let us count the ways.

"Every important turn on my writer's path has been preceded by unhappiness," Nancy admits. "The more major the turn, the worse the misery. I left regular paying jobs in order to be a freelance writer because I was miserable working full-time for other people. I started writing poetry because of the sadness I felt over a miscarriage. I left freelancing to write fiction full-time when I became miserable doing commercial work. I quit writing a successful mystery series in order to write something new because I was miserable after ten books in the old series. I even uncovered these seven steps because I was so thoroughly sick of hearing myself say the same old things at writers conferences that I found myself thinking harder and digging deeper."

Nobody likes to listen to a writer whine.

"But I'm not through yet," she insists. "It isn't just the major career changes. I'm always restless and anxious

How's that working for you?

—Dr. Phil

before I start a new novel or short story. I can be perfectly happy doing nothing for a while, but then it starts to build up, until I can't stand it, and I *have* to write. At some point, the anxiety turns to eagerness, and then I can't wait to sit down and start."

She's not the only one. This phenomenon appears to be normal, or at least what passes for normality among writers. When novelist and short-story writer Lia Matera goes through periods of restlessness and anxiety, she uses them to paint—but not as a way of avoiding her feelings or avoiding writing. In fact, she uses painting as a way to find her way back *into* her writing and maybe even create some positive memories for the future.

"It's a funny thing, how many interesting memories can come out of the restless, depressing times between decisions or courses of action," Lia confides. "I think sometimes that the most sensible thing to do while enduring them is stuff you know will strike you as interesting in retrospect. I call my theory of disappointment management *Be Here Later*. Those activities might be ashes while you do them, but retrospect is most of life. There might not be a lot of ways to make this time suck less while you're in it, but there are ways to make times more interesting to look back on. That's why I start painting.

"When I paint, I feel as if I should be working on a book instead. I have ideas, I have places I could begin, ways I could start, even if not at the beginning and even without quite knowing what I'm after or where I'm going with it. But I don't want to write only because I need the money. I want the work to be separate from fear and obligation. I find that I can't bear not to create something (which I didn't really know about myself until I tried this), so instead of turning on the laptop, I pull out the paints. Because I'm not a capital-p Painter, and it's very unlikely that there's any way into a career in painting, my painting is just about painting, about expression and vision and trying to capture something worthy, even if it's not what I visualized when I started. But I see myself improving at this, and it reinforces my feeling that when the writing is also all about the writing, and nothing else, that's how it should be. I have this idea that by working this way, I will find my way to a different and fresher and more generous feeling about writing."

"*. . . I can't bear not to create something . . .*"

Lia has just articulated the heart of this step. It's the "can't bear" part of it that leads to the "create something." She's a good example of doing step one the right way, even though what she's doing doesn't look like writing. But then, she's a pro, and she knows what to do when the feeling hits her. She lets her restlessness or anxiety lead her into other kinds of creativity rather than just sitting and feeling miserable or trying to force her writing out too soon. Even though her route of creativity is of a different sort than writing, she's doing it *for* the writing, and she's in no way avoiding her true feelings.

It takes a lot of courage to endure all of these uncomfortable feelings. It's one thing to ride them out in some interesting way; it's another thing entirely to sedate them, drown them, drug them, or otherwise try to kill them. We live in a smiley-face culture that tells us that all we need is one more affirmation, an exercise class, or a pill, and then everything will be hunky-dory. But that's not the "culture" in which a writer lives. We have to exist in a different state in which sometimes we must allow

Fear is the dark room in which negatives are developed.

—Anonymous

our anxiety and restlessness to build to an almost intolerable level without trying to make it go away.

When it builds up enough steam, it will drive us to writing.

Success is simply a matter of luck. Ask any failure.

—Earl Wilson

Feeling and Revealing

Feeling your way through this step is vital, but it isn't all there is to it. In addition to allowing yourself to experience the full extent of how miserable it can get to be in step one, you'll also benefit from *revealing* what you're honestly feeling, instead of running from it or hiding it, especially from yourself.

Lynn had this experience of feeling and revealing while working on this chapter.

"I sent a query off to someone about a new book idea, and he told me in so many nice words, 'No way, José,'" she says. "I thought I had evolved to the point of not letting these little rejections bother me, but unfortunately, I hadn't. I spent the evening imagining myself giving up writing completely, reminding myself that I can't write worth a plugged nickel. I pictured myself broke, living out of my car while traveling around the U.S., not working or writing for a year. Then I woke up and started in on my current book."

Lynn did exactly what she always tells her clients to do: feel it. She also *revealed* it to a writer friend. That friend didn't tell Lynn she "shouldn't feel that way." She mirrored back to Lynn how bad it really did feel, without minimizing it. That helped Lynn to accept it and move on. That's the beauty of revealing our true feelings to somebody we trust. It's comforting to have our feelings "legitimized" by somebody besides ourselves. Writers groups frequently perform this function for their members. They're where you can go to unload how anxious you feel, when nobody else wants to hear it and nobody else can really understand.

Nancy remembers when she tried to go for the Guinness record of not feeling or revealing, because she didn't know how to do it.

"Once, I was horribly blocked on a book for many months," she says. "In hindsight, I can so easily see that the problem was that I was hiding from the unhappiness I was feeling about other things in my life. But instead of just going ahead and *feeling* those things, I tried to distract myself by getting immersed in other activities. I fell in love with papermaking, then I became a birdwatcher, then I learned all about mushrooms." We call that *make-work*—which rhymes with fake work—or a big, long *break* from work. "I was creating happy memories, as Lia so wisely recommends, but what I wasn't doing was facing how unhappy I really was. This required speaking out loud to someone what I had been reluctant to say. When that finally did happen, my life turned around literally overnight. I went from feeling depressed and sluggish and unproductive one day to feeling healthy and full of energy the next. It was amazing and instructive. Not long after that, I was writing again."

That's the power of feeling and revealing, as anyone in a twelve-step recovery program will tell you. And don't worry about dissipating your creative tension by talking about it. As members of twelve-step programs can also testify, letting the lid off of your unhappiness is much more likely to free your creativity than to stifle it.

Many writers can attest to the huge payoff for suffering through the initial tension this step represents. Bestselling author Nora Roberts says writing is "better than sex." Mystery author Margaret Maron says it's "better

No sleep comes to me in all those dark hours.
—John Wesley Powell

than sex and chocolate." But to get to that happy ending, you've got to be willing to feel the frustration and tension that precede it. Some people find that nearly unbearable to endure.

"Before I was a writer," says Gary Legwold, "was I ever unhappy. I thought I'd love to be a writer, but I left teaching and went to carpentry, which lasted two weeks, and then to landscaping, which lasted a summer. I was still miserable, so on a fluke, I went to a newspaper and said, 'I've always wanted to write. Do you have a job for me?'"

Amazingly, they did. It was his frustration that finally moved him.

Allow yourself to get miserable and maybe unhappiness will move you, too.

It moved Jonathan Franzen during the god-awful days when he was writing his future best-seller *The Corrections*. In a long and excruciatingly revealing interview with the author, *The New York Times* reported on his days that "simply vanished." They fell into a black hole of "solitary hands of bridge, idle fiddling with power tools, gratuitous afternoon naps. There were evenings that disappeared as well," the article went on to say, "washed down with shots of vodka and followed by sleepless nights. There were flashes of inspiration succeeded by months of despair." A typical day for him was, "Awful, awful."

You're still sure you want to do this? Good. Then let's continue.

It is only by expressing all that is inside that purer and purer streams come.

—Brenda Ueland

Now for the Bad News

You've heard, or maybe even experienced for yourself, what it's like to feel the ordinary creative urge, but what is this step like when it's very, very hard? We've already given you a glimpse of it, but here's a fuller look.

It's like when you're completely miserable in your current job and you'd give everything you own to chuck it all and write for a living. It's like when you've had writer's block for so long you've forgotten which goes first, the subject or the verb. It's like when you've finished a draft of a novel, and it reads like crap, and you're exhausted, and the idea of rewriting it fills you with despair. It's like when your proposal has gone to twenty editors and the answer is still "No," and you don't know whether to scrap all your work or dig up the energy to try again. It's like hell on flat wheels.

"When I think of this step at its very worst," Nancy says, "some famous paintings come to mind, like *The Scream*, by Edvard Munch." You know the one—there's a wavy, distorted view of a pier, and at the front of the picture, there's a man with his mouth open, and you can almost hear his scream. "That's a picture of this step at its worst," she says, "and I'm not exaggerating. I suspect that poor ol' Edvard had been here once or twice himself. Or how about Vincent van Gogh's famous painting *Potato Eaters*? It's just awful. It's this dark, dreary picture of peasants who are eating the only food they've got. Not to equate writing with the plight of nineteenth-century Dutch peasants, but I've felt that way before I get an idea—dull as dirt, hungry for something better, and stupid as a potato." And then, just to expand on her theme, there are those famous sculptures by Michelangelo—*The Captives*. They're four naked men,

Pioneers may be picturesque figures, but they are often rather lonely ones.

—Nancy Astor

hideously and eternally caught in marble. This step feels just like *that* sometimes, too. When it does, you'd give anything for Michelangelo to come around and release you from the stone.

Isn't There Any Good News?

We've already hinted at the good news: the purpose of steam is to make a kettle sing, the purpose of an itch is to make you scratch, the purpose of emotional fuel is to drive you forward in your life.

If an itch gets bad enough, you *will* scratch it, unless you've tied down your own hands in some way. Even if this step goes way beyond a mere itch, even if it hurls you down to the very bottom of the pit of unhappiness or discomfort or fear, that's where things can begin to turn around again in the most amazing way. Where it's darkest, that's where van Gogh comes in with his paintbrush heavy with yellows and oranges, and Michelangelo begins to chip away the stone. Way down here, in the place of sighs and tears and discouragement, of irritability and aggravation, of sleepless nights and pacing days, that's where the sun of creativity shines in. This is where discomfort turns into eagerness to write.

Sometimes, scratching these itches can lead to life-changing events.

"I had a miscarriage around Christmastime when I was thirty-four," Nancy says. "Afterward, I told everybody I was fine. Three weeks later, I went skiing. I cried all the way down the slopes that first day, but I figured it was only because I was out of shape because of the pregnancy. 'Are you OK?' people asked me. 'I'm fine,' I assured them, and I really thought I was. But one year later, on a day when I was Christmas shopping, I suddenly felt an overwhelming urge to sit down on the curb of the busy street and weep. I couldn't imagine what had come over me—until I remembered it was the anniversary of my miscarriage. In that instant, I realized I had repressed and denied all of my sorrow. This time, as I let myself feel all of it, within days it mysteriously transformed into an impulse to create poetry, and so I began to write.

"My poetry writing turned into writing short stories within a year, and a few months after that, I was writing a novel. I'm convinced that my creativity emerged directly from my sorrow. If I had never felt all of that unhappiness, I don't know when—or if—I'd ever have found my writer's path."

A similar transformation happened to Steve Dixon, who grew unhappy at the height of his career as an attorney. He was doing so well that he owned his own office building and had the largest complement of attorneys and support staff in the county. But Steve says he got tired of making his living from other people's misery.

"Suing people doesn't bring them happiness and joy," he says. "People coming to a law office are not having fun."

After several attempts at other ventures, after the end of his marriage and the end of his law partnership, he decided to look for joy and to reframe and renew his life. He bought a sailboat and began adventure sailing and cruising the islands of Hawaii, and he began writing about it. Steve is now living on his boat and telling his stories.

Sometimes, unhappiness provides an even more direct route to writing than it did for Nancy and Steve. It

I like living. I have sometimes been wildly, despairingly, acutely miserable, racked with sorrow, but through it all I still know quite certainly that just to be alive is a grand thing.

—Agatha Christie

begins to look almost like therapy. Novelist Judy Goldman says that when both of her parents were dying, "I took to my typewriter instead of my bed. I wrote and I wrote. It's what saved me."

As with almost anything, using writing to express pain can sometimes turn into almost too much of a good thing, as poet Jose Climent testifies:

"I had to face the beast," he told us, referring to certain dreadful, even violent, occurrences in his life. "I couldn't look it in the eye because it was too devastating, so I sublimated the pain by making it beautiful by means of poetry. I can point to every page in my book where I was lying, putting a good face on something by using so many beautiful words and so many ways around it."

As writers, as people, we do the best we can in our particular circumstances. We feel as much as we can tolerate. We write as truthfully as we have it in us to do. The important thing to remember when unhappiness visits you is to let yourself feel it as completely and honestly as you can, to tell the truth about how you're feeling, and then to allow it to lead you toward your own individual expression of creativity. Perfection is not in the cards in this step, or in any of the other steps. You'll do the best you can. In hindsight, Jose may feel less than satisfied with how well he dealt with his unhappiness, but we think he did a heroic job with step one.

Writing saves lives, expresses lives, changes lives.

It's no wonder, then, that strong feelings come with this path. And that really is the good news, just as we said earlier, because the stronger the itch, the more likely you are to scratch it.

This stretch of the river is named Hell's Half-Mile.

—John Wesley Powell

Other Signs That You're on This Step

Boredom is a dead giveaway to the probability that creativity is lurking in your psyche. When Lynn's clients complain about feeling bored, she tells them to get up and dance a jig. When they hear that, some of them take offense. They think she's crazy or teasing them or just not taking their problems seriously enough. But Lynn knows that their boredom is a hopeful sign, because it's the harbinger of their creative process. It's a symptom that couldn't be more clear if they walked into her office with spots all over their face. Something is starting to incubate in them, and if they ignore it, it's only going to get worse.

No doubt, they—and you?—could relate to Si Morley, the hero of the classic science fiction–mystery novel *Time and Again,* by Jack Finney:

> In shirt-sleeves, the way I generally worked, I sat sketching a bar of soap taped to an upper corner of my drawing board. The gold-foil wrapper was carefully peeled back so that you could still read most of the brand name printed on it; I'd spoiled the wrappers of half a dozen bars before getting that effect. This was a new idea, the product to be shown ready for what the accompanying copy called, "fragrant, lathery, lovelier you" use, and I had the job of sketching it into half a dozen layouts, the bar of soap at a slightly different angle in each.
>
> It was just exactly as boring as it sounds, and I stopped to look out the window beside me, down twelve stories at Fifty-fourth Street and the little heads moving along the sidewalk. It was a sunny, sharply clear day in

And when I'm not working, I'm not working at all, although during those periods of full stop, I usually feel at loose ends with myself and have trouble sleeping.
—Stephen King

mid-November, and I'd have liked to be out in it, the whole afternoon ahead and nothing to do; nothing I had to do, that is.

That character is ripe for something new. He's bored with his life. "Excellent," Lynn might say, if he were a client of hers. He's allowing himself to feel all of that boredom. Even better. And he's saying it out loud, to us, the readers. Good for him. That deeply felt and acknowledged boredom makes him fertile ground for wanting the adventures that are about to happen to him next, just as any boredom you feel and reveal makes you ripe for something new, too.

Did you know that Agatha Christie grew to loathe her character Hercule Poirot? She was *bored* with him, so bored she killed him off, no doubt with great pleasure. Imagine feeling that you must continue writing book after book about characters you've grown to hate. Boredom can descend upon even the most successful writer. In fact, sometimes it's the most successful ones who have the hardest time owning up to these feelings, because the idea of telling their agents and editors that they don't want to do it anymore is very threatening to them and to the people who depend on them. What if they don't know what they'd do instead? What if they do something else and they fail or don't reach the same level of success as before? They can linger forever in a kind of rich, successful purgatory that nobody in his right mind would ever envy.

While we're in this emotional swamp, let's not forget loneliness. Just as boredom is a sign that your psyche wants to get creative, loneliness is a sign that you're missing something. Could it be your good friend writing? In Annie Proulx's Pulitzer Prize–winning novel

For me, not working is the real work. When I'm writing, it's all the playground, and the worst three hours I ever spent there were still pretty damn good.

—Stephen King

The Shipping News, there's a wonderful description of the loneliness and confusion of a man who doesn't even know that he will soon become a writer: "Nothing was clear to lonesome Quoyle. His thoughts churned like the amorphous thing that ancient sailors, drifting into arctic half-light, called the Sea Lung; a heaving sludge of ice under fog where air blurred into water, where liquid was solid, where solids dissolved, where the sky froze and light and dark muddled."

Ever feel like that yourself? In the novel, Quoyle's loneliness and confusion set him to searching, though for what, he didn't even know. But because he felt it deeply and followed where it led him, he ended up in happier and more creative circumstances. He didn't just remain stuck where he was, denying how bad it felt, instead of moving in the direction it took him.

Any loneliness and confusion you feel can lead you, too.

And then there's anxiety, another form of unhappiness and a sign that points to incipient creativity. All writers feel it at one time or another, some even as deeply as Harry Potter does, in *The Goblet of Fire*, when he's worried about the novel's bad guy, Voldemort: "Harry went restlessly back to the bed and sat down on it, running a finger over his scar again. It wasn't the pain that bothered him. Harry was no stranger to pain and injury. . . . No, the thing that was bothering Harry was that the last time his scar had hurt him, it had been because Voldemort had been close by. . . ."

For some writers, the approach of change and creativity has that same touch of dread and doom to it, as if their own Voldemort were haunting them. *The writing . . . is close by.* Margaret Maron knows that feeling. She says, "I can feel it in the underbrush, moving toward me like some wary creature, but I know it'll eventually step out of the trees." If you feel anxious about the prospect of writing, at least know that your creativity is out there, waiting for you.

Everything looks impossible for the people who never try anything.
—Jean-Louis Etienne

There can be feelings of apathy and lethargy, of depression, and of hopelessness to this step. Feelings of helplessness, in other words. That's because, when we're in it, we tend to hope for a while that something external will jolt us out of it or save us from it. We're like Adam on the ceiling of the Sistine Chapel, listlessly lolling around until lightning strikes. We're like a damsel tied to the railroad tracks. We're a cork floating in the ocean or a swimmer caught in the breaking surf and getting slammed again and again onto the bottom. We daydream that someone will save us by coming along with a great idea or a job offer, a proposal, a movie deal, or scissors to cut us loose from the railroad tracks. Hey, it could happen. But usually, we're on our own, because if there was ever such a thing as an inside job, it's unhappiness.

"I tend to feel the most unhappy," Lynn says, "when I perceive that something's out of control and there's nothing I can do to make it better, like when I'm waiting for my agent to call me back and tell me if she likes my new proposal. Or when I think I've done a good job on a chapter and my editor says it's not quite right and I don't have a clue how to fix it. At those times, I can get like a sad little robot whose battery has almost run out, and the best I can do is just let myself be absolutely miserable for a little while until I fall over in a heap. When I catch on to what's going on with me, then the worst is over and I rise again, with renewed energy and creativity. Suddenly, I know how to fix that chapter. Or suddenly, I get busy with other things and stop worrying about when my agent will call. But I have to catch it—and be willing to feel how unhappy and out of control I feel—before that transformation can happen."

Feeling precedes the transformation into action.

Still Not Convinced You're Ever on This Step?

By now, you probably have a pretty good idea if you are on this step, or have ever been on it, but some people wouldn't acknowledge anything like unhappiness if it came up and knocked them in the head, which eventually it will if they continue to repress and deny it.

"Whose unhappiness is that?" we might ask them. "Is it yours?"

"Mine? Heavens, no, I've never seen it before. It's not mine. I don't know whom it belongs to, but it's certainly, definitely not mine."

Sure, and that's why they're sick or moping around like sad pups.

If you are one of those hardheaded diehards, here's another way to find out if you're on this step: check in with your thoughts, your feelings, or your actions.

Thoughts, in case you don't listen to them very often, are what go through your head, like these: "I feel so dry and lifeless." "Everything feels meaningless." "There must be something better in life than this." "There must be something more interesting for me to do with myself. I'm so bored!" "It's the same ol', same ol', and nothing ever changes." "I think I'll die if I have to keep living like this." "Maybe I'm depressed. Maybe I have an anxiety disorder. Maybe I'm crazy."

Feelings, just in case you have denied them for so long that you're oblivious to them, are those sensations

Everyone has talent: what is rare is the courage to follow the talent to the dark place where it leads.

—Erica Jong

you get inside your body, and we're not talking about indigestion or hunger pains. Most of them can be found below the neck. One word is usually enough to describe them: *anxious, itchy, frustrated, bored, restless, sad, despondent, tense, unfulfilled, fearful, despairing, ashamed, unhappy, miserable, uninspired, stuck, unenthusiastic, irritable,* or *hopeless.*

If all else fails, and you can't tell if you're unhappy, then try taking a good long look at what you are actually doing. If you sabotage yourself, trudge, procrastinate, give up, talk a lot but don't do anything, read but don't write, even though you think you want to, go to conferences but don't write, even though you intend to, hide your pain from other people, isolate yourself, or get physically ill, then you qualify for the label "unhappy," and for this step.

The worst part of it is the anguish that precedes the act of writing— the hours, days or months when we search in vain for the phrase that turns the spigot that makes the water flow.

—Octavio Paz

But what if you let yourself feel those ways, and it's uncomfortable, and you're tempted to go back to denying, distracting, or repressing your unhappy feelings? Here's an idea that Lynn recommends to her clients when they start to leave the path: When you're so itchy or unhappy or full of creative tension that you could burst, and you're tempted to give up on step one, just pretend you have a sheepdog who's nipping at your heels. His job is to keep you on track when you falter. So when you start falling into a really bad attitude about how you feel—when self-pity begins to tug at your sleeve, for instance—let that sheepdog keep you on the path. Listen to him. He's barking some really good advice at you. *You're just having a feeling, that's all. It will pass. It won't kill you. This is a temporary situation, not your whole life. You're not alone. Boredom and unhappiness have been the beginning of the creative process for many people . . .*

Yip, yip, yip. Restrain the impulse to kick him. Instead, keep your heels out of his teeth by putting one foot in front of the other, and then keep moving. In fact, it's a good idea to literally move your body. Get up. Get out. Walk, swim, do some yoga. Or do something creative that's different from what you usually do, as Lia does— write in a journal, paint a picture, take guitar lessons. Let that sheepdog help you keep your perspective on life, on your feelings, on writing.

This is only one step, remember, not the entire path.

Welcoming the Dark Guest

Writers who handle this step well don't need a sheepdog. They know better than to pretend they aren't having these feelings. But what if they masked their feelings, sedated them, or distracted them? It would be hard to blame anybody for doing that because, after all, this hurts sometimes, and we're used to spraying an analgesic on raw cuts. But they don't do that. They feel the pain; they let it bleed. After all, there's a good reason for that old adage "Writing is easy. Just open a vein."

What if you opened the vein but then stanched the flow?

Trying to pretend this step isn't happening or attempting to push your way through it, like pushing cheese through a sieve, only leaves you with that shredded feeling. The people who will eventually be writing are those who choose the path of actually feeling whatever level of discomfort they have, enduring it all the way through, until at last it emerges as an urge to be creative.

When writers get really good at this step, they can even use it to feed their process.

"If I'm about to start a book," says Trish MacGregor,

There was a period of four to five years where I didn't write very much. It wasn't a happy time for me and I had feelings of restlessness, the innate feeling that there is something I had to do with my life that wasn't being accomplished.

—Jeffrey Marks

who writes both fiction and nonfiction as T. J. MacGregor, "I try to spend a day or so *not* starting it, letting the creative adrenaline build. Then when I sit down, stuff pours out."

To pull off that trick, the writer's got to be able to tolerate an increasing inner tension that may not feel very good while it's happening. Trish can do that, because she has forty books and thirty years of experience to guide her. It's a real challenge for beginners, though, and for people who aren't willing to feel tense or itchy. If you're in either of those categories, maybe it will help you to know that a measure of initial discomfort is a natural part of being creative. The more willing you are to put up with it at the beginning, the sooner you will be able to start to write.

It's our observation that most people—the ones who aren't writing—either don't know this is required or aren't willing to do it. It's way too uncomfortable for some people. They aren't out there dancing that recommended jig, welcoming those feelings of boredom, and so forth. Instead, they are medicating those uncomfortable feelings with alcohol or drugs, with sex or shopping, with television or hobbies they don't really care about, or with jobs whose only purpose is to keep them from thinking and feeling.

Yes, we know it's scary. A writer may be afraid that if she lets herself feel as unhappy as she really is, she might then feel as if she has to make some kind of painful change in her life. But like Persephone in the Greek myth, sometimes we've got to descend into Hades before we can come up for the harvest.

Damn. This step doesn't sound like much fun, does it?

That depends. We know a poet and journal writer, Richard Keith, who revels in his own misery when he feels it coming on. He even takes pride in it. Here's a wonderful poem he wrote that metaphorically portrays himself, the artist, as a host and his own loneliness and unhappiness as a guest:

No less than a Turkoman village headman am I obliged to
   show courtesy and hospitality to my guest,
even this dark guest of emptiness doubt and despair.

You get the idea to welcome the dark guest one time, check
   him out,
serve him chai in a chipped ancient glass cup passed from
   Bedouin hand to Bedouin hand and thence to Persia, Hazara,
all the way here and suddenly the dark guest is softer than you
   ever thought possible.

He shocks you, bestows vast unexpected wealth on you.
No one has ever merely sat with him, silent and formal and
   courteous, crossed legs on carpets in a mud brick Turko-
   man hut.
No one has ever just accepted the risk, even prescribed by the
   Koran, to welcome and show hospitality to the dark guest.

Alas brave village headman, there is such melancholy here.
You will lose the dark guest that only now you learned to love.
Your hospitality transforms him.

He will return.
But each time he calls in his wanderings he will be less dark.
He will grow soft, radiant, joyous.
There will never be another dark guest as dark as he who first
   you risked all, welcoming quietly and abandoned of hope.

Mark well this first visit.
Years hence you will cherish it.

The keenest sorrow is to recognize ourselves as the sole cause of all our adversities.

—Sophocles

If you think about creativity as being a form of birth, then it makes sense not only that there will be labor pains but that they can—in theory, at least—be greeted "bravely and with joy," as the samurai recommends. Novelist Sally Goldenbaum says that when she had her children, she actually welcomed the painful contractions. "The worse they got," Sally says of her labor pains for three babies, "the more excited I got, because I knew I was getting that much closer to having a child."

When unhappiness is the precursor to creativity, it's a good thing, a natural thing.

So if you're undergoing "labor pains," it means there's writing on its way. For some of us, it'll be a mercifully quick labor and delivery; for others of us, or at other times, we may have to set endurance records. But fast or slow, hard or easy, there's some tension and pain that precedes creativity.

Being perfectly happy rarely creates that kind of tension. How could it?

"Gosh, I've got millions in the bank, a beautiful wife, three perfect children, my dream house on the Riviera, sexual and emotional satisfaction, thrilling intellectual challenge, spiritual fulfillment, and I can hardly get to sleep at night, because I'm so excited about the idea of waking up to a new day in the morning. So I think I'll change."

That person will never write a single word, not until a touch of unhappiness and dissatisfaction creeps into his life.

When the well's dry, we know the worth of water.
—Benjamin Franklin

One Last Word about Unhappiness . . .

In the arc of your life, you'll revisit this spot on the trail many times.

During the writing of this book, Lynn's mom, although she looks as if she's fifty, turned eighty and suffered a debilitating eye condition. When Lynn asked her what that was like, Shirley demonstrated a way to handle this step through acceptance.

"My life has gone from active to inactive," Shirley told Lynn, revealing her feelings with total honesty. "My future looks bleak and boring, and not a place I'm excited to go. I'm not saying I want to stay in this state forever. I break it up occasionally, take a trip, do something, visit an old friend. I know the way out of this place is by accepting things the way they are, because I know I can't change them. Healthwise, my body has deteriorated. My parts got old and they aren't replaceable, so I need to find new activities to brighten up my life."

Like Lynn's mom, you can control acknowledging where you are at this moment in your life (revealing) and accepting that you feel the way you feel (feeling). You can't control *that* you are here or *what* you feel. You *are* here, and you *do* feel.

What you can control is how you think about being here.

People who want to be writers, as opposed to people who actually write, often seem to believe that becoming a published writer is all they need to make them happy at last. Well, if that's what they want—to be published—then it probably will make them happy. For a while. It certainly makes us happy when it happens to us. But the writing life, like any other one, can bring great

The greatest mistake you can make in life is continually to be fearing you will make one.

—Elbert Hubbard

unhappiness, too. When our first drafts stink—as first drafts do—are we happy about that? No. When we pour our hearts into our writing and then it gets rejected or gets a bad review, are we pleased? God, no. When we write really hard and then the book, the article, the poem gets stuck, are we thrilled? No, we hate it. There is no permanent state of happiness in writing. But neither is there a permanent state of unhappiness—unless you never get through this first step.

Argue for your limitations and sure enough they're yours.
—Richard Bach

As a writer, under normal circumstances, sometimes you will feel overjoyed and sometimes you will feel despair. Sometimes, writing will feel so good that you'll fool yourself into thinking you've got it licked and that now you'll be happy forever. Enjoy it while it lasts.

"But why can't it last forever?" you whine.

Because it can't, that's why. Because it won't, because it never does, because you would never write another thing if it did. Here's what would happen. You would finish whatever it is you're writing, and then you'd be so content that you'd never need to pick up a pen or move a mouse again.

"Sometimes, that sounds pretty good to me," Nancy confessed to Lynn one time. "Sometimes, I think I'd trade it all in for constant happiness."

"But without writing," Lynn pointed out, "you wouldn't be happy."

"How do you know that?"

"Have you ever tried not writing?"

"Yes."

"Were you happy?"

"At first, I was. I gardened; I painted my dining room; I took piano lessons. I had lunch with a different friend every day. It was really fun. I loved it."

"How long did that last?" Lynn asked.

"Oh, maybe three weeks," Nancy mumbled.

"Uh-huh. And then how did you feel?"

"Unhappy."

"How unhappy?"

"Eventually? Really unhappy."

"What was that like for you?"

"It was like, what do you call it? Hell. I couldn't sit still, but I couldn't think of anything I wanted to do. I got anxious, twitchy, grouchy, sad, depressed. I was a mess."

"So what did you do then?"

"I bitched about it."

Lynn laughed. "And then what did you do?"

"I wrote."

"And how did you feel then?"

"Happy."

Unless you're an enlightened master, there's no such thing as a constant state of happiness or unhappiness, not even as a best-selling writer. Perhaps we should have told you to sit down before we broke this news, but we think you'll just have to take it like a grown-up instead of like a writer. Writing will not permanently cure the blues. Becoming a "real writer" will not enroll you in heaven on earth. You'll work harder than ever; you'll still get frustrated and bored and unhappy now and then. Writing is not to be confused with undying bliss, though you may feel blissful sometimes, too. Here are some of the times when you, as a writer, may have to endure some degree of unhappiness along this path: when you start out, when you veer off, as you do the work, when you finish it.

And sometimes, you might even get stuck here. How will you know?

For one thing, it will go on for a long time, maybe

even years. You'll find yourself reworking the same novel—or the same sentence—again and again, like Oscar Wilde, who said, "This morning I took out a comma and this afternoon I put it back again." Or you'll become a regular at writers conferences, without ever finishing enough work of your own. You'll realize one day that you've been talking a good writing game without actually doing it. Maybe you'll come across a list of ideas you once jotted down, and you'll realize with a pang that you never wrote any of them. Maybe your writer friends will progress while you're left behind. And maybe this has happened to you only because you're stuck in the tension of step one, a tension that can be released only by feeling it fully.

Do that, and the moment may come when you feel like the young werewolf in *Blood and Chocolate*, by Annette Curtis Klause:

> Suddenly she craved the change.
>
> Her laugh turned to a moan at the first ripple in her bones. She doubled over as the muscles of her abdomen went into a brief spasm, then grimaced as her teeth sharpened and her jaw extended. She felt the momentary pain of the spine's crunch and then the sweet release. . . .

We never said this step was easy. But ah, the sweet release. This dramatic transformation will happen for you when you reach the absolute end of step one, which is when you can say with finality, "I don't want this anymore." Great!

Now, then, what *do* you want?

Wanting

Step Two on the Writer's Path

• •

If you ask me what I have come to do in the world, I who am an artist, I will reply: "I am here to live aloud."

—Émile Zola

What's money? A man is a success if he gets up in the morning and goes to bed at night and in between does what he wants to do.

—Bob Dylan

Did your wanting get you to pick up and read this book? Our wanting certainly got us to write it.

"Do you *want* to write a book with me?" Nancy asked Lynn.

"Yes, I *want* to," Lynn responded eagerly.

"Do you think any publisher will *want* it?" we asked our agents.

"Who will *want* to read it?" publishers inquired of our agents.

It was wanting that got us here, and now you're here, too. It's a little embarrassing, all this unabashed longing. Well, let's make this real clear: you'll never write unless you want to. Want. Want. Want. Want. There, we've said it, that *nasty* word. You've got to want it, want it, want it, want it. Even if wanting it makes you feel bad for a while, even if you stand a good chance of not getting what you want, even if you suffer for it, even if other people suffer for it, you've got to want it, or you may as well just forget it. Does that sound tough? We're sorry if it does, because we don't mean to scare you, but we also have to tell you, that's how it is. If you *don't* want it enough, you definitely won't get it. Trust us on that much, at least. If you do want it enough, at least you stand a fighting chance of getting "it," whatever "it" is for you. For us, it means writing and publishing again and again. We want that, WANT IT, and would shout that from the rooftops if that's what it took to make it happen.

WANT. WANT. WANT. WANT. WANT.

Whether in fiction or in real life, there's nothing so powerful as desire.

That power is exactly why a lot of people are afraid of it. They're afraid of feeling it in themselves, of saying it out loud, of acting on it, or of being around other people who display it openly.

In her other life, Lynn is a psychotherapist. For the last thirty years, on an average of four days a week, she has sat in her office listening to people who are struggling with being human. Mostly, she says, what they're struggling with is wanting. They want to feel better. They want their children to behave better. They want their spouse to be different. They want to understand why their lives aren't how they pictured they'd be. They want to know why they feel so depressed and blue and sad and angry and so on. A lot of them are artists of one sort or another, including writers.

All that wanting may not be a pretty thing in their mirrors, but it's a beautiful thing from a therapist's point of view. "Without it," Lynn says, "my clients would still be sitting home doing more of what isn't working, and feeling awful. It's their wanting that gets them to my office."

Interestingly, she has found that unhappiness alone won't do that for them.

> *Luck is a matter of preparation meeting opportunity.*
>
> —Oprah

"Before they pick up the phone to call me for an appointment, before they get behind the wheel of their car or ask somebody else to drive them, they've got to want something, even if it's only to feel better tomorrow than they do today."

They come looking for their destination in life, she says, not even realizing that their unhappiness and their longing have already put them on the path to it. She tells them their wanting is their North Star.

Like the North Star, our wanting is a beacon that shows us our way. When we feel lost on this or any path, all we have to do is look down at the compass of our wants and begin to move in that direction. We are convinced that when you're stuck, wanting will get you unstuck.

And It's No Different for Writers

The rest of the world tends to think writers are special, which is probably a dangerous attitude for a writer to buy into. "I don't know how you do it." "I could never do that." "I wish I could do what you do." Apparently, what we do looks mysterious to people who don't do it, and our lives look enviable—all that supposedly free time with nothing to do but be wildly creative. Little do they know the truth, right?

Maybe it's OK for the rest of the world to think we're special, but it's deadly for us to believe that, because if we do, we also lose ourselves as writers. Distressing as this is to admit in public, we are just like everybody else, except, perhaps, for our facility with words, and even that is just a talent, a skill, an ability. Apart from that, God knows we get just as unhappy as anybody else does, and we love things, hate things, want things, and don't want

It's so hard when I have to, and so easy when I want to.

—Sondra
Anice Barnes

things as much as anybody else does, too. But because the writing life is supposed to be special, prized, exclusive to a fortunate few, it's tempting to forget there's an ordinary human being underneath all those clever words, a person with all the wants and needs and difficulties accessing them as anybody else.

All things considered, maybe it's just as well that most writers also hold other jobs. With that kind of overawed attitude abroad in the world, it's probably a good thing that most of us still have to earn a regular paycheck somewhere else or change dirty diapers, sweep the kitchen floor, and do the laundry. While we're working, teaching, sweeping, cleaning, we can think about our wants.

When Wanting Is Working

It sounds so simple. All you have to do is want. But it must not be that simple in real life, or else why wouldn't more people be writing what, where, when, as much, and as well as they want to? Instead, they're still languishing in a state of unsatisfied desire. They're stuck back in step one, Unhappiness, and they can't seem to get out of it, no matter how bravely they face it or how honestly they acknowledge what they want from writing.

The trouble may be that most of us tend to assume that wanting is only about feeling, that it's just about intense pining, longing, desiring for something such as writing or for being a best-selling author. Conventional wisdom these days seems to preach that if you only let yourself want something enough, you'll get it, and that strong feeling and affirmations will do the trick. Certainly, depth of desire is a part of the answer, and there's nothing wrong with doing affirmations, but what we're missing when we stop there is the second part of want-

Just don't give up trying to do what you really want to do. Where there is love and inspiration, I don't think you can go wrong.

—Ella Fitzgerald

ing, the action part that Lynn's clients learn to do. We call that part focusing and collecting. Before we show you how to focus and collect, both skills that can be learned, we'd like to show you what it looks like to want something as much as it takes to get it.

Consider Stephen King, who said in his own book about writing, "At thirteen I wanted monsters that ate whole cities, radioactive corpses that came out of the ocean and ate surfers, and girls in black bras who looked like trailer trash."

That's honest, that's wanting, and look where it took him. We don't think anyone was saying to Stephen, "Honey, it's not nice to think about corpses and monsters and trailer trash. Can't you focus on something more important?" If he was getting that message, he didn't let it get in the way of his wants.

When Kevin Robinson was a young man, he dived into sparkling blue water, broke his neck, and became a quadriplegic. Years later, his extreme disability didn't stop him from passionately wanting to be a published writer. Using the two fingers he could move, Kevin wrote three novels that were accepted by a major publisher. If someone told Kevin he had to give up being a writer because of his disability, he certainly wasn't listening or taking them seriously. And he wasn't letting his accident become an excuse for not trying.

That's wanting, and look what it accomplished for him, despite "impossible" odds.

Professional writers constantly hear would-be writers say, "I'd write, if I only had the time." No they wouldn't. Time has nothing to do with it. Martha Powers used to put her children to bed at night and then write from 10:00 P.M. until 4:00 in the morning. When Julie Garwood's children were small, she made herself get up and

Nothing contributes so much to tranquilize the mind as a steady purpose—a point on which the soul may fix its intellectual eye.

—Mary Wollstonecraft Shelley

start writing every morning before her family woke up. Nancy started her second book three weeks after her baby was born, going down to her basement office to write whenever he "went down" for a nap, keeping a monitor nearby so she could hear if he cried. If you want to write, you do what you have to do to make it happen, whether you have the time or not, and whether you have the energy or not. It's wanting that drives you to make the time; it's wanting that gives you the energy.

Kevin Robinson is living proof of that, as are the other writers to whom we spoke in the process of putting this book together. They write between jobs. They write between babies. They write in five-minute dabs and five-day marathons. They write when they can, where they can, as they can, but they write, regardless of whether they have the time to do it. They make the time, every time, because they want to, and they want to *enough*. What is "enough"? Enough is however much it takes.

Do you allow yourself a mild kind of wanting, a faint glowing instead of a radioactive desire? Then you're probably going to mildly get what you want, a little taste instead of a satisfying meal. Do you allow yourself to want a little stronger than that? Then you're likely to get a little more of what you want, but not a whole lot more. Do you let yourself really want it on Monday but then reprove yourself for being selfish on Tuesday? If so, you're probably going to get what you want only sporadically, if at all.

Or do you want it so much that your desire could eat whole cities?

Then you're likely to get what you want in a big way or go down in flames trying, but at least, you'll never have the regret of *not* trying.

I was always looking outside myself for strength and confidence, but it comes from within. It is there all the time.
—Anna Freud

It's not about time, and it's not about energy.

It's not about inspiration, either. Some people think their creative process begins with inspiration, but we think otherwise. We think that although they may not know it, by the time they get to inspiration, they have already done a lot of traveling down the creative process, and that it's the covering of all that earlier ground that allows them to be inspired. Some of them have fulfilled their inspirations so often that they don't even appreciate how well they do it or that not everybody is as adept as they are at taking the steps that lead to inspiration.

As Bob Dylan said in the opening quote, it's also not about money. If it were, there wouldn't be all those stories of starving artists and of writers scrabbling any way they can to make enough money to support their writing habits.

In fact, too much time, energy, inspiration, or money can be as debilitating as too little of it, so don't try using any of those as your excuse, at least not around writers who don't use those excuses. Plenty of writers have carved out whole days to write, only to find themselves staring hopelessly at a blank page that refuses to be filled. And if you want to appreciate the curse of too much energy, try taking cocaine for a few weeks and see how creative you are then. Inspiration, too, can be a curse for writers who have more ideas than execution. As for money, there's nothing like a rich income to really kill the creative urge in some people. When Nancy was twenty-six, she quit her well-paying corporate job, because she was scared of getting trapped by the "golden handcuffs" of retirement packages and group insurance. She took off on her own, starting a freelance career in which "I earned exactly half as much money, worked twice as hard, and had three times as much fun."

All I can do is act according to my deepest instinct, be whatever I must be—crazy or ribald or sad or compassionate or loving or indifferent. That is all anybody can do.
—Katherine Hathaway

"To be truly challenging," Sterling Hayden wrote in his book *Wanderer*, "a voyage, like a life, must rest on a firm foundation of financial unrest. 'I've always wanted to sail the South Seas, but I can't afford it.' What these men can't afford is *not* to go. They are enmeshed in the cancerous discipline of security. And in the worship of security we fling our lives beneath the wheel of routine. And before we know it our lives are gone."

Under the wheels of routine is where Jay Gatsby certainly never threw his life. And that's one of the reasons why, seventy-six years after the first publication of *The Great Gatsby*, a panel of writers, poets, critics, actors, and publishing officials voted him the greatest literary character of the twentieth century. Seventy-six years! What is it about Gatsby that gives him such a lasting hold on our hearts and minds? It can't be just that the book is still read in high schools. There must be more to it than that, or there wouldn't still be teenagers declaring that *Gatsby* is their favorite book. Why does this character continue to strike such a powerful chord with readers? It's because he *wants*, he *longs* and *yearns* with an aching fierceness. Jay Gatsby knew what he wanted and went after it, "at an inconceivable pitch of intensity," as F. Scott Fitzgerald wrote of him.

But What If Wanting Isn't Working?

We're frightened by what makes us different.
—Anne Rice

Novelist and nonfiction writer T. J. MacGregor confided how she feels the creative itch and then purposefully lets it build until it practically explodes her into her office, like a human cannonball, ready to start writing. Oh, to be so clear. For many of you, your ability to want may be buried deep, and all that shows on the surface is an indefinable longing. You sense you want something, but what is it? What would get rid of the itch, the ache, the angst? Wanting is the one emotion that seems to require a pickax, a miner's lamp, and a shovel to bring it to the surface.

Why is that? Because wanting, like unhappiness, has got a bad rap in our society. You're not supposed to want anything. That would be selfish; that wouldn't be nice. God forbid you should desire something with every fiber of your being. That would be downright unenlightened of you. Does any of this sound familiar to you . . . ?

> *I'm not sleepy! I don't want to go to bed!*
> *It's late, and you have to go to bed now.*

> *I don't like peas! I don't want to eat them!*
> *You don't know that. Try them, you might like them.*

> *I don't like this dress. It's ugly.*
> *No, it isn't. It looks pretty on you.*
> *I hate it.*
> *No, you don't hate it. Just try it on . . .*

> *I want to go to the movies tonight.*
> *Well, you can't, and that's final.*

Et cetera. Your wants: o. Your wants squashed: 1,300,064 by the time you're ten years old. We start out saying what we want, and then we hear the word *no*, in a thousand different forms, over and over. We start out saying—clearly!—what we don't want, and we get told it doesn't matter, again and again. Is it any wonder you lose the ability to know what you really want or don't want? Is it any wonder you get scared to ask? Is it any wonder you feel defeated before you even try?

I want to do it because I want to do it.

—Amelia Earhart

We're not saying those are bad parents who say such things. This isn't about blame, because that would get you nowhere fast. What we're saying is that a million transactions like that have the ultimate effect of squashing your honest feelings of want/don't want. They get flattened by "no" and "don't be silly" and "you can't." They get steamrollered by shoulds and musts and other people's expectations, not to mention all the life obligations you load upon yourself before you know what you really want.

Haven't we all heard that desire is the root of suffering? Well, yes, *unrequited* desire is, but desire fulfilled? What's that like? That's like happiness, at least until the next time you get restless and itchy and what you have attained no longer satisfies you, but then that's the human condition. We want; we go after what we want; if we're lucky, it satisfies us for a time; and then we go after something else. Do you think that's a bad thing? We think that's a natural thing. You want to eat, you eat, and later, you want to eat again. This is bad? You get tired, you want to rest, you sleep, you get up, and eventually, you want to go to bed again. Shame on you? We don't think so. The sea "wants" to ebb and flow, flowers "want" to bloom and die, and writers want to write, and then they want to stop writing, and then they want to write again, and then . . .

Get rid of desire? We may as well speak of getting rid of oxygen, because both are fuel for our lives, oxygen and desire. Without them, we're either dead or may as well be. If you're an enlightened master and you truly "want for nothing," that's one thing, and more power to you. But let's be honest here. Neither of us is an E.M. Are you? Didn't think so. That being the case, hold on to your hats, because we're going to be talking about passion here—unadulterated, balls-out, full-throated, unashamed *passion* for living and writing.

We all know, or have seen, people with a lot of want/don't want power, and we also know that "it offends some people and scares the shit out of others," as Lynn bluntly observes. "They get criticized for being too definite, too ambitious, too sure, too bossy. They may be those things, but I don't necessarily see those as liabilities. What I've noticed is that some of those same people are also the very ones who will bend over backward to help the rest of us get what we want, if we're as clear about it."

That tends to be true of people who follow their own North Star and have their own compass pointed in the right direction: they have enough self-confidence to help you line yours up straight, too. On the other hand, we all know people who drive everybody crazy by trying to be "nice." They just won't say what they really want, even about something so simple as picking a restaurant or a day on which to meet. They may also encourage you to do what you want, but there will be an undercurrent of resentment if that isn't what they secretly want as well. Wouldn't it be "nice" if just once they would cheerfully and unapologetically say, "I want this."

But then, of course, they might not get it, and there's the rub.

It's also another reason why you may have turned off your want motor or kept it at a low idle. When you know what you want, you have something to lose, like Gatsby or like any writer who has ever sent out a manuscript. That's why it's so daunting to admit what you want, because then you might have to go after it, you might never get it, you might get more than you bargained for, or you might have to give up whatever it is

Duty is an icy shadow. It will freeze you. It cannot fill the heart's sanctuary.

—Augusta Evans

you don't want anymore. In fact, if the idea of wanting to write—or of wanting to take the chance of writing something new, different, or more challenging—spooks you, it's not too late to back out. Now's your chance. You could take the wry advice of J. G. Ballard, who warned would-be writers, "A lifetime's experience urges me to utter a warning cry: do anything else, take someone's golden retriever for a walk, run away with a saxophone player."

Do anything, in other words, instead of writing. After all, according to writer Thomas Mann, "A writer is somebody for whom writing is more difficult than it is for other people." Now's your chance to leave the writer's path without dishonor.

If you're still with us, know that wanting is gutsy, visceral, not dainty, pretty, polite, proper, or socially acceptable, at least not when it shows its teeth. But it's also rugged, strong, out-there, honest, and it can be as attractive as all get-out, in more than one sense of that word.

It is an *attractive* power, which means it attracts to it the things or people it needs in order to be fulfilled. It's like a magnet. The stronger the magnet, the stronger the pull; the weaker the magnet, the weaker the pull, and it's judgment-neutral, which is to say that it operates if you want something that's good for you, and it operates just as well if you want something that turns out to be bad for you. Look where wanting got Gatsby, for heaven's sake: he lost the girl and got murdered in his own backyard. Not a very good advertisement for desire, you might say. It's no wonder a lot of people are wary of it.

But "not wanting," which is really wanting something else in disguise, is really *unattractive*. What does it look and sound like? It's pretty pathetic. Its voice may be

Even I don't wake up looking like Cindy Crawford.
—Cindy Crawford

a monotone, or dry and whispery, or brittle and too perky by half. It sounds depressed, uninterested, martyred, uncaring, defeated, or frighteningly chirpy. It says, "I don't know," "I don't care," "You choose," "I can't decide," "It doesn't matter," "I don't mind," "Whatever you want is fine with me," and "It's not important anyway." It looks like head down, eyes dull, caved-in shoulders, down-at-the-mouth. It walks with a trudge, slumps in its chair, leans its face on its hand, stands with its hands in its pockets, and watches too much TV or sleeps too much. It could reside in a writer who is blocked or who has been beaten down by the publishing industry or one who either doesn't know what she wants to do next or doesn't quite want it enough to get going on it.

"Not wanting" comes with two very smelly by-products called resentment and lethargy. It schlumps around filled with the noxious, poisonous gas of resentment. It has given up or been defeated or never really got started in the first place. It does what others think is best for it, instead of what it most deeply wants to do with its life, and it doesn't see any way out of its dilemma. And then there's lethargy, the passivity of "not wanting." It's enough to make even you sick of yourself. It feels like a victim; it bores itself to death; it's sick a lot. What it is, is wanting turned inside out, and it eats you up from within.

Enough, already. It's miserable to read about, worse to endure.

And exactly what difference does any of this make to your writing, and why are we going on and on about this? Because if you can't generate the fuel of desire in this step, you'll never be able to fully commit yourself in the next one. Then, somewhere along the line, you'll run

I don't know what I think about certain subjects, even today, until I sit down and try to write about them.

—Don DeLillo

out of creative steam and sadly, helplessly, angrily wonder why. If that happens, *this* is why: you ran out of want power.

Let's Get Those Motors Running

If you are feeling frustrated, that's a dead giveaway that you aren't doing what you want and instead are probably doing what you think you should, must, or have to. Time to start wanting. We guarantee that it's a myth that if you do what you want, everyone will hate you and that you'll turn into a wild animal, wreaking havoc and destruction wherever you go.

If you know what you want, commit to it and start doing it. Some writers claim they begin their process already on step two, wanting to write, without ever having to do step one. We suspect the truth is that they move so fast through step one that it doesn't even register with them. If they ever wanted to check that out, all they would have to do is stop themselves from writing when they feel the desire to do it. Most likely, they would quickly feel all the itch and unhappiness that somebody on step one could ever feel, and then they would realize it was there all the time. They were just lucky or experienced enough to whiz through it. No two writers go through these steps at the same pace, and we can experience them differently on any given writing project. There are countless times when writers slide right through this step with no problem at all. They feel a creative itch— the low end of the unhappiness scale—and then they quickly realize what it is they want to write in order to scratch it. No problem. But as is the case with all of these steps, sometimes the process is not nearly so easy. Sometimes it's downright agonizing, and it can drag out for

It's all right to have butterflies in your stomach. Just get them to fly in formation.

—Dr. Rob Gilbert

years or even for a lifetime of half-baked misery. Nevertheless, the steps are always there, underlying and guiding our process. If you ever doubt it, just try stopping yourself in the middle of any one of them.

If you're not having any trouble feeling the itch and know what you want to write, you may want to skip on over to step three, and we'll meet you there. But if you're stuck in a morass of not-writing and not being committed to your writing, the rest of this chapter is for you.

It is curious how a little obstacle becomes a great obstruction. . . .
—John Wesley Powell

Collect and Focus to Find Your Wants

If you don't know what you want, or if you aren't sure, try our simple suggestions for collecting and focusing. Collecting is the process of gathering all your current wants together in one basket regardless of how badly you want them or how much you are willing to do the work to get them or whether they are any of your business in the first place. Without identifying your wants, it would be difficult to focus in and prioritize what you are going to commit to in the next step on the path.

Here's the easiest way to get to your wants. Write the words *I Want* at the top of a page. Then, without stopping to think, fill the page with the "I wants" that stream out of you. Let yourself go. Have a blast! Don't stop to make judgments or berate yourself or worry about what your mother might say or feel guilty or silly or correct your spelling. Just let 'er rip. "I want this, and I want that, and I also want that, and besides that, I want that over there . . ." Remember, just because you write it down doesn't mean you have to actually get any of these things. You're only making a list to see what comes out of you. You're safe here, and nobody else ever has to know. When you run out of ideas, put the paper aside, preferably where nobody else will see it. It's none of their business, unless you *want* to make it so.

Tomorrow, pick up your "I Want" page (or pages!), read what you wrote, and then start adding more to the list, beginning with, "And in addition to what I already wrote, I also want . . ."

Do this for a week, and you will see patterns begin to emerge.

If "I Want" scares you too much, try "I Wish" instead. You can wish for anything you like; it doesn't mean you have to get it or do it. After a few days of wishing, maybe you'll feel bold enough to use the *want* word.

If doing the "I Want" pages seems like too much effort, here's a quick 'n' dirty version called the "I Want Fingers." Hold both of your hands out in front of you and imagine placing an "I want" on each of your fingers. Do it fast, without thinking. When you get to the last ones, you may be amazed by what you say. You may discover wants you didn't know you had, and they will probably be the important ones, more important than the first seven or eight that rolled easily off your tongue.

When Nancy tried this, she said for her first finger, "I want a good man," and laughed out loud. Then she said, "I want a happy and satisfied life for my son." At that point, she looked over at Lynn and asked, "Does it count if I want it for other people?" Lynn said, "Don't think. Don't censor. Just want. Keep going." So Nancy continued, ticking off financial security, a house on the ocean, a house in the mountains, world peace, an end to hunger and suffering for all children, a snappy new car, bestseller status for everything she writes from here on out, and number ten, to be of profound help to her readers. As predicted, that last one shocked her, because she hadn't seen it coming at all. Her list might be different tomor-

The major job was getting people to understand that they had something within their power they could use.

—Ella Baker

row or a week from now, but at this moment, she has easily taken the pulse of her wants and zeroed in on her top priority.

That's what this step is all about—getting crystal clear on what you want.

And here's another idea, if you're not sure you fully did the work of the Unhappiness step. Try doing some "I Don't Want" pages or "I Don't Want Fingers," and see what you find out about what is making you unhappy or would make you unhappy. We think that if you were to do all of these exercises, in fact, you would be crystal clear as a mountain lake, and then all you'd have to do is decide whether or not to dive in.

Diving in is the way you focus your wants. When Lynn cooks, she collects ingredients and recipes until she has to make a decision. Even as she begins cooking a meal, she's often not sure what it will turn out to be, but she has at least narrowed down the ingredients. That piece of salmon may end up in a pasta, a risotto, or on the barbecue, but salmon it is.

Listen to the Tongue in Your Shoe

You can always tell where a person's focus is if you watch his or her actions, and you can tell where your focus is by looking at your behaviors. Think about it. There's a tongue in your mouth and another one in your shoe, and it's that second one that will tell you the truth about what you really want. It speaks the language of the body, and the body never lies about what we really want.

Lynn has observed this lie detector in her writing partner.

"When Nancy and I are writing in the same location, and both of Nancy's tongues are speaking as one, here's

I was sitting in a bookstore signing my books and someone asked me if I'd always wanted to be a writer. At the moment it struck me that I was indeed a writer.

—Barbara Seranella

what it looks and sounds like. Nancy says she's going to write. Within minutes, she's sitting on the couch with computer in lap, writing. There's not an ounce of pro-crastinating. But I've seen her tongues tell conflicting stories, too. When she first said to me, 'Let's write a book together,' a year later, we were still sending E-mails back and forth. There was no writing going on, because she didn't really want to yet, no matter what her mouth was saying."

The mind-body connection is all about congruent and incongruent messages.

We all know people who say they want to write, for instance, but who seem to do everything *but* write. There's Rachael, who says she wants to write, but then she volunteers to spend two weeks at a church camp, and as soon as she gets back from that, she invites her old college roommates to a reunion weekend at her home, and she takes her grandkids on trips, and she takes pi-ano lessons, and ... Her mouth is saying, "I want to write," but her feet take her where she really wants to be. Oh, she may feel guilty and unfulfilled about not writing, and she may complain to her husband and her friends that she never gets time for herself, but it's *her* body that's showing up at church camp and those piano lessons, not theirs.

One of the quickest ways to become exhausted is by suppressing your feelings.
—Sue Patton Thoele

Then there's Paul, who says in March, "I want to write a chapter a week, and let's see, I can start the third Friday in July ... Oh, no, I think we have a baseball game that night ... So maybe the first Monday in Octo-ber? No, that won't work either ..."

You can see what Paul really wants, and it isn't to write anything right now.

Does your body show up at the computer or at the TV? It knows how interested you really are. Does it pick up the phone whenever it rings, or does it turn on the answering machine so that you can't be interrupted while you're writing? It knows what you want. Does your mouth say yes when the Heart Drive calls asking you to volunteer, or does it say no, because you want to write?

Does the tongue in your shoe call the one in your mouth a liar?

Try this collecting and focusing activity if you can stand it: either think about, or actually take a piece of paper and write down, what your mouth has been saying about your writing intentions the past day, week, month, or year. What have you said you were going to do? Then think about, or write down, what your body has actually been doing during that time. Compare the two—and take a good look at what you really want. It's all there, isn't it? If you have been saying you intend to write but your body has been avoiding it, the message is that you don't want it enough to actually do it. (And remember, no excuses about time, money, responsibilities, health, or energy here.) If, however, both of your tongues have been saying the same thing, then you're actually walking your talk. Clearly, you *do* want it enough to actually do it.

If you don't like what you are learning about your own habits, hang on, because by collecting this information about yourself, you're already on the way toward changing the picture to something you may like better.

I have been very greedy. I wanted it all—a regular life and a writing life, and somehow I've managed to get it. I was never aware of sacrificing anything, but my husband and son might have a different take. I may have sacrificed their wants and desires.

—Margaret Maron

Be Open and Ready When You Stumble into Your Wants

As a beginning fiction writer, Nancy almost immediately got some of what she wanted, enough to fool her into thinking it was going to be easy.

"When I started out," she continues, "I hit it lucky right away. I got the first agent I approached. I sold the first short story I sent out. I thought that publishing was going to be easy and that I had it made. Then came a year and a half of rejections on my first novel and on my short stories. I grew frustrated, angry, unhappy. I felt stymied, but I wanted it enough, and my wanting was strong enough, that I kept plugging away at it. But even after I got several novels published, I still couldn't seem to sell a short story for love nor money. I kept reading other people's short stories, looking for some kind of answer as to what might be wrong with mine. And then one day, my wanting, which was fueling my intense work and my searching, hit pay dirt."

She went to a one-day writers conference at William Jewell College, in Liberty, Missouri. It cost her ten bucks, including lunch. It was there that she heard a published short-story writer, Gladys Swan, say that every short story needs an epiphany. That would have been old news to creative-writing students versed in Aristotle and James Joyce, but Nancy was self-taught and didn't know that. She realized in that instant that her failed short stories were gimmicky, plot-driven, and lacked any change in the characters, and she hurried home to remedy that failing.

"The next story I sent out was accepted for publication."

T. Jefferson Parker stumbled pretty gently into what he really wanted. He says that when he was in the tenth grade, he loved reading *Catcher in the Rye*, and he decided that someday he wanted to write something that might give other people at least one one-thousandth of the pleasure it gave him. That's what he thought he wanted. But years later, when he started writing his first novel, *Laguna Heat,* he became enthralled with mysteries.

"I liked the dark underbelly," he said during a speech a few years back to the San Diego chapter of Sisters in Crime, "the sleazy people smiling on the outside and plotting terrible things on the inside. The incest, greed, dishonesty, and all that stuff. I thought it was just tops."

Someone less honest with himself might well have squashed those feelings. He might have reproved himself, saying, "That's not nice. That's not literary. You shouldn't write about such nasty things. You should only write something that will be classic literature."

Well, it just so happens that T. Jefferson Parker writes beautifully and with literary merit in his chosen field of mystery and suspense, and so he has managed to have it both ways: write well and write what he loves best. But if he hadn't followed his wants, and then been willing to listen to his even deeper wants, he'd never have discovered that great talent in himself, and neither would his devoted readers.

Lynn remembers a time when she gently stumbled into her wants, too.

She had taken a summer job as a camp program director when her kids were four and two. Until she started working there, she didn't realize how confined her life had become or how much she missed working. She loved being a mom, so she had felt fulfilled, and she forgot that that was only one part of what made her a whole person. The creativity she used at the camp felt very different from what she'd been using at home, however, and it felt wonderful. Suddenly, she stumbled across the realization that she missed working, she missed that part of herself, and she wanted to work again.

> *The hardest thing to learn in life is which bridge to cross and which to burn.*
>
> —Laurence J. Peter

What if Lynn had ignored that stumble? In that case, the next message might have been a harsher one, as it was for thriller writer John Lescroart, when he was forty-one, published, but not yet making a living at it. One day, he took a break to go bodysurfing at Seal Beach. The next day, he lay in a Pasadena hospital with spinal meningitis from contaminated seawater. The doctors gave him two hours to live. His eleven-day battle with death was the turning point that changed his career forever and got him in touch with what he really wanted. He quit his day jobs, moved back to northern California, and started writing full-time with a new intensity and direction. It took a disaster to wake up, and heat up, his wanting, and John would probably be the first to say, "Don't try this at home."

Establishing goals is all right if you don't let them deprive you of interesting detours.

—Doug Larson

Instead, listen to your earlier warning systems, as Nina Osier managed to do.

Nina Osier turned forty before she realized that something was missing from her life. She had given up writing in her twenties, because all she got were the *good* rejections. Her "spring" dried up. One day, while she was being interviewed for a church newsletter, the interviewer asked her, "What did you dream about doing when you were eighteen? Have you done it yet?" Nina answered, "I dreamed I'd be a published science-fiction writer by now." Once she said that out loud, her restlessness got worse for several months, and then she started writing again.

Cecil Murphey is another writer who listened to his wantings, even though they meant he'd have to make a dramatic change in his life. "I spent more than a year working toward my doctoral degree," he says. "Shortly after I started the second year, I became increasingly dissatisfied and bored—the first time I had not enjoyed college or grad school. I heard about a ten-week course on writing for publication. The next week, I dropped out of the doctoral program and have felt no regrets. I've made my living as a full-time writer since 1984."

Heed the Messages
of Your Dreams and Nightmares

Sometimes, your dreams take over the job of pointing out your wants to you, as they did for Nancy. Years ago, she was close to agreeing to write a freelance project for two men who said they couldn't pay her anything until after the whole thing was finished. They seemed so nice, they were so enthusiastic, and the project seemed so worthwhile, that even though it would be a financial hardship for her to do it, she was close to signing a contract for it. She felt uneasy, but she ignored that honest thought and the feeling of unease in her body. "I didn't really want to do it," she remembers. "I wanted to turn them down, but I thought I should take the job because it was for such a good cause."

The night before she would have signed their contract, she had a dream of a landscape full of snakes in the grass! Next day, she told them no. It was no surprise to her—or to her subconscious—when she learned a year later that their project had failed and some people didn't get paid. She could have been one of those people if she hadn't listened to her dream. But Nancy wouldn't even have had to experience such a frightening dream if she had been willing to listen to herself in the first place. The truth was, she didn't want that job; she did want jobs that paid her at least enough to live on.

If we fail to heed the messages that our body, dreams, or fantasies are trying to get across to us about what we

Discipline is remembering what you want.
—David Campbell

really want, life will find other ways to get our attention, sometimes gently, sometimes more forcefully, and sometimes with a wicked sense of irony.

Speaking of irony . . .

I'm So Jealous I Could Want

What would you say if we told you that jealousy, envy, insecurity, and self-pity are four of the best traveling companions you'll ever have? What if we even went so far as to suggest that you let them lead you through this step on the path?

No, we're not crazy—at least, not at this particular moment. We know that those unpopular feelings will tell you what you really want. You can take it from us, jealousy and envy are feelings that say, "I want what *they have!*" Insecurity whispers in your ear, "You're not good enough unless you have what they've got." And self-pity whines, "Everyone has what you want." Just as a red face tells you that you're embarrassed and tears tell you that you're sad and laughing tells you that you're having fun, these feelings tell you what you desire most. They help you start collecting information about what you want, kind of like putting wildflowers into a basket. Some people will call your "wildflowers" weeds. Let them. We're here to tell you they will make a fascinating bouquet. Whether you like it or not, whether your mother would approve or not, they will tell the truth about you. They will tell you what is important to you, and they will rise straight up from your gut, where wanting lives.

Envy, jealousy, self-pity, and insecurity. They are your goal-setting feelings. Isn't that a hoot? But it's true: they will help you to brainstorm your true priorities—

A man begins cutting his wisdom teeth the first time he bites off more than he can chew.

—Herb Caen

not the ones you *think* you have, or think you *should* have but the ones you really do have so you have a collection to choose from and focus in on. Right now, those true priorities may only be unconscious within you, but we're going to make them conscious now, maybe for the first time in your life.

Get ready for some surprises about yourself.

Goals are dreams with deadlines.
—Diana Scharf Hunt

Lynn and Nancy's Jealousy, Envy, and Longing List

Yes, we'll show you ours so you don't have to feel embarrassed to show yours. Deal? Once you get into this, it's kind of fun, as well as being productive.

So here we go.

Lynn says, "I'm jealous of Robert B. Parker, and I envy his ability to paint a complex picture with a few broad strokes, and I long to write like him. I'm also jealous of Barbara Kingsolver, and I envy her ability to say so clearly and poetically her views on women, issues that I have written about and talked about for years with much less eloquence. I long for the voice to evoke deep feelings while entertaining my readers with Kingsolver's understanding, humor, and honesty. I'm jealous of Colin Fletcher's intensity and focus, and I envy his trip down the Colorado River, and I long for a time when I can take a six-month road trip and write about it. I'm jealous of Dennis Lehane and Martha Grimes, who can paint pictures with words. I'm jealous of all those writers of self-help books who capture millions of readers with a single phrase like 'who stole my cheese' or 'feel the fear and do it anyway.'"

Are you getting the picture? By welcoming her

feelings of jealousy, envy, and longing, and writing about them, Lynn is able to see more clearly what her current wants are, which are really her current priorities.

This is what that list said to her about her priorities: "I want to write better. I want to find my voice. I want to create time for an extended travel period that includes travel somewhere wonderful and exciting. I want to create a book that's witty, wise, and warmhearted and could sit on every bookshelf in the world."

Now for Nancy's jealousy, envy, and longing list.

"I'm jealous of the way Louise Erdrich ties short stories together to make wonderful novels. I'm jealous of how Alice Hoffman uses magical realism to create a fictional universe that includes the otherworldly as well as the worldly. I'm jealous of how Susan Isaacs and Lia Matera can write funny. I'm jealous of how lovingly J. K. Rowling has created the details of the world of Harry Potter, and I'm jealous of how unhesitatingly she goes to extremes in her writing, hanging right out there on the edge, particularly in regard to violence, without seeming to care what the critics will think, and I'm jealous of romance writers who get to write explicit sex scenes. I envy anybody who gets to write a script for *Buffy the Vampire Slayer*. In fact, I'm jealous of anybody who writes about vampires or werewolves. I'm jealous of anybody who writes a magical adventure yarn like *Lost Horizon*, *Lord of the Rings*, or *Raiders of the Lost Ark*. I'm jealous of really smart science-fiction writers. I envy anybody who never has to worry about money, and I envy people with long, happy marriages, and I envy anybody who ever got to dance with Fred Astaire. Actually, it is Fred himself who I always wanted to be when I grew up, not his partners."

What great thing would you attempt if you knew you could not fail?
—Robert H. Schuller

That's Nancy's envy, jealousy, and self-pity list. But what does it mean?

"If a stranger had written that," she says, "what would it tell me that she wants to write? I would surmise that she wants to write both short stories and novels. She wants to write with wit and style (Fred Astaire). She wants to take chances (J. K. Rowling's going to extremes, 'on the edge') but from a nice, secure base (the 'long, happy marriage'). She wants to write fantasy adventure stories that are funny, sexy, exciting, bloody, mysterious, and spiritual ('otherworldly'). In addition, I'd say that she wants to lead the way and step forward rather than backward (Fred Astaire again). She's not likely to want to write historical novels."

Twenty years ago, Nancy might have filled in all the blanks with the names of mystery writers. She might have said she was jealous of Agatha Christie, James M. Cain, Robert B. Parker, John D. MacDonald, Ngaio Marsh, Margaret Millar, and so forth. Her priority was writing and selling mysteries. She moved toward what she wanted then, but now it's twenty years later. She has an established career as a mystery writer. She has done it. Now there are other things she wants that she doesn't have.

An amazing thing happened to Nancy the day she finished writing and thinking about that list, the kind of "amazing thing" that does happen when we face the truth about ourselves. That night, she suddenly got an idea for a fantasy/adventure story for young adults, a novel that could give her a chance to revel in all those things she envies other people for doing. Will she do it? She knows she wants to, really wants to, but she has other deadlines, other writing she "should" do first— enough to keep her away from this great new idea for

After a good drink, we walk out to the brink of the canyon, and look down to the water below. I can do this now, but it has taken several years of mountain climbing to cool my nerves, so that I can sit, with my feet over the edge, and calmly look down a precipice of 2,000 feet. And yet I cannot look on and see another do the same. I must either bid him come away, or turn my head.

—John Wesley Powell

years, if she lets it. Nancy knows that not every want ends up being an "I'm going to," but it's great to have a full dance card—to know there's more where the last idea came from, when she's ready.

We never stop wanting. At every stage of our writing lives, it's our wanting that moves us to take the step of serious commitment to getting what we want. It's what keeps us growing and thriving. It's what puts us on the writer's path to begin with and keeps us there. But what if you *think* you know what you want and you *think* you're going after it, but it keeps hanging out of your reach, no matter what you do?

What If I Never Get What I Want?

Ah, yes, that's always the danger, isn't it? Not getting what we want. Well, what of it? Isn't it worse never to try to get what you want? And anyway, some of the emotions that assail us when we don't get what we want are the very ones that can motivate us to go back and try harder or better.

Like anger, for instance. It's a good sign, because it shows you're wanting.

Contrary to what you may have heard, there are no negative feelings. There are simply feelings. We think that using your envy and jealousy and self-pity and insecurities to zero in on what is really important to you is a great gift and time-saver. Anger is another so-called negative feeling that is a big helper on this step. You'll definitely feel it if anything or anybody gets between you and what you want. Writers who are trying to get published know exactly what we mean.

"I've been there," Nancy says. "I know that after you've sent out your stories, poems, articles, or books, and all you've got back are form rejections, it begins to get you sad *and* riled. What's the matter with those stupid people in New York that they can't see the value of your work? Why won't they accept you?"

A few years ago, Nancy found a journal she had written during her first year as a full-time fiction writer. During that year, she sold the first short story she wrote, she finished a novel, and got the first agent she approached. Fiction looked easy; life felt grand. But then nothing else happened for what seemed to be forever.

"My novel was rejected by one publisher after another," she recalls. "Nobody wanted any of my short stories, either." For a year and a half, Nancy's new life as a full-time mystery writer, the one she had created with so much joy, excitement, and gratitude, felt like nothing but writing and rejection.

"Afterward, I was able to remember how hard it was," she says now. "But until I found that journal, I had completely forgotten my anger. There's one point in the journal where I say, 'I'm so sad and I'm so angry'— complete with exclamation point—'I'm so angry!' When you want to be published so much you could die, and you're trying so hard, it just kills you when nobody wants you. And remember, I'd been a professional writer for years. I was used to acceptances, not rejections. I was even used to being paid, of all things. What a concept. All that ended when I started writing fiction.

"The journal reminded me of the unpleasant truth that I had spent a year and a half whining, bellyaching, and stomping around in an absolute fury. Normally, I don't think of myself as an angry person. But I was then, when I was on step two. I felt so bitter. Why couldn't they see that I was a real writer? Why couldn't they see that I was a *good* writer?

"It was only later that I understood that when I started my fiction career, I was, theoretically, a 'good' writer, but that I was still learning how to write fiction. Those editors who rejected me were seeing work that wasn't ready for prime time yet, but I didn't know enough to realize that. I only knew that I wanted, I wanted, I wanted. I was a big ball of want. I was *so* frustrated, so angry, so humiliated, and so very, very sad."

Does that feel familiar to you?

If so, just know that you're still on the path, and take some comfort from that. If you're angry about not getting what you want, that's an excellent sign that you actually know what you want and are trying to get it, which is a whole lot more than most people can say, so good for you.

But what if you know what you want, or think you do, and you still can't seem to work up the energy or motivation to go after it? Where does the "enough" of "wanting it enough" come from?

For some writers, just facing their own true desires does the trick.

The trouble with not having a goal is that you can spend your life running up and down the field and never scoring.
—Bill Copeland

If it doesn't for you, you may need to prime the pump. If you've done the exercises in this chapter and you've had an "aha" moment about what you want, start collecting information and feelings about it. Tell good friends or understanding family members about it, and put it out into the universe. Talk it up. Start reading true-life stories of people who have accomplished great things in difficult circumstances. Find some heroes to be your mentors in how to get what you want. Collect photographs and make drawings that depict your heart's desire. Do affirmations. Write your "I Want" list ten times every day. In other words, start making it visible instead of leaving it in your head. When one of the early winners of the *Survivor* television show won the million-dollar prize, she said she had "always" known she would, and that weeks before she was even selected to be a contestant, she had put a winning message up on her computer at work so she would see it every day.

If your motor hasn't been running in the right direction for a long time, it may take you a while to get it turned around and headed the other way toward what you want. Expect that. Work on making your wants visible, little by little, step by step, until you actually start to feel the deep motivation and eagerness that will lead you into the next step, which is the commitment to doing it.

How will you know when you've done this step "correctly"?

You'll know because you won't be able to help wanting what you want. You'll want it so much that you won't even ask the question. You'll just want, that's all. In the same way that feeling the itch or unhappiness explodes you onto step two, so it is that your wanting will push you powerfully along your path into making a commitment.

Commitment

Step Three on the Writer's Path

• •

"Frank, what do you think this whole thing will cost?"

"I'm guessing it will come in at about half a million."

*"Well, if you want, you've got yourself a partner," Dick
said, extending his hand. Frank smiled; if there was anything
he liked it was a man willing to make up his mind quickly,
and taking Dick's hand he said, "You're on."*

—Dick Bass and Frank Wells
  with Rick Ridgeway, *Seven Summits*

Here is an excerpt from the diary of the explorer John Wesley Powell on the day he launched the first exploratory expedition down the Colorado River in the Grand Canyon:
*"May 24, 1869. We raise our little flag, push the boats from shore, and the
swift current carries us down."*

Imagine that—with sheer walls rising on either side of them, and a
violent river surging ahead of them, they set out on an incredibly dangerous journey that no one had ever taken before, not even the Native
Americans who had lived throughout the territory for centuries.

The small group of onlookers who waved and cheered good-bye
to ten men in four boats at Green River Station, Wyoming Territory,
in the late spring were seeing commitment in action. This was the
end of the planning that began when John Wesley Powell scouted the
Green River in January of the same year, and the real beginning of
his trip to the foot of the Grand Canyon. It ended thirteen weeks
later, but Powell's diary indicates there were many moments when it

was far from obvious that the trip would end in success or that there would be any survivors to tell about it.

When those ten men pushed off from the shore, it was their moment of commitment. If you've ever traveled the Green or the Colorado, you have some idea of what was ahead of them, once they entered the current. Although no one could predict the outcome, no one could deny that they were on their way. Powell's group understood commitment: if you don't step into the current, it can never carry you.

One hundred and thirteen years later, another group of adventurers who understood commitment gathered at a retreat center on the verdant banks of a big, calm pond in northern Kentucky. On the day this band of thirty writers "launched" their expedition, they faced no literal waterfalls, no raging white water, no cliffs, no grizzly bears or mountain lions. This was only going to be a weeklong writers conference. The most dangerous creatures they would face were the big, fat woodchucks and the Canada geese.

These thirty were explorers of a different sort—our kind, the writerly kind. They were doctors, physicists, teachers, computer technicians. They were two pilots, a clergyman, and at least one housewife. They worked in insurance and in law. Some could easily afford the considerable expense of the retreat; others had saved or worked harder or gone into debt to pay for it. They were black and they were white. They were old enough to be retired and young enough to stay up all night. The important things they almost all had in common were that they had felt how unhappy it made them if they didn't write, and then they had let their desire to write grow until it gave them the courage they needed to make this grand commitment to their writing. They took the risk

It takes five years to break in and fifteen years to be able to support yourself as a writer.

—Sue Grafton

and gambled big on what they wanted. For ten glorious, hard, demanding days, they laid down their money and their time on the table where their wants were. They, too, stepped into the current so it could carry them.

With the power of conviction there is no sacrifice.
—Pat Benatar

Unhappiness leads to wanting. Wanting leads to commitment.

"I want to write," every single one of those writers had been saying for a long time. But unlike many others, those participants in a ten-day writers school and retreat actually showed up with their bodies and their minds to do what they claimed they longed to do. It wasn't fancy there at the retreat center, but for once in their lives, they had everything that writers dream of having: time and space and unconditional support from everybody around them.

They had no excuses left, in other words.

They had little rooms to themselves, they had their computers, they had classes to attend, agents to meet, editors to whom to show their rooms. The communal areas chattered with talk and bubbled with laughter, but the long corridors remained thoughtfully quiet as they tiptoed past one another's work. Books were born, or torn up and begun again, or nearly finished. Careers started or were revived or rethought that week. They had POS buttons to wear anytime they fell into a funk and thought their writing was a "piece of shit," and the buttons signaled that they needed pats on the back, hugs, and encouraging words. They were served food, somebody else washed their sheets, but they did their own heavy lifting where the writing was concerned. They wrote. For those ten amazing days away from their "regular" lives, they became the full-time writers they longed to be.

It wasn't cheap, and it wasn't easy, but what meaningful journey is?

Have you ever longed to give your whole heart and soul to something as they did, as John Wesley Powell and his little band of explorers did? Have you ever wished you could take a risk—any risk—as brave and adventurous people do? Have you ever gazed at people who seem to be committed to something as if their lives depended on it and envied them?

If so, then what you're wishing for is the courage of the same kind of commitment those writers have, the courage to step into the current of *your* river so it can carry you. When the longing of wanting turns to making decisions and taking action, you are clearly on the third step on the writer's path, right along with John Wesley Powell, the band of thirty at the writers conference, and anyone who has passionately lived the creative process.

Imagine their faces, the focus and determination in their eyes, the set of their mouths, the courage and hope in their hearts. What you're seeing in your mind's eye is the picture of commitment. Is that what you want, too? Do you long to feel that deeply, to care that much, to be that committed and passionate about your writing, whether it's a commitment simply to write or a commitment to write a particular thing? Do you want to care about what you write? Most of us do. Do you want to feel your commitment to it so deeply that you can be sure—as sure as anyone can be—that it will carry you over the hard parts to your goal?

If it's commitment you want, you've come to the right place. You have reached this point by feeling the full extent of how unhappy it makes you not to write and then by allowing yourself to build up the steam of *waaanting*, until it's so powerful that you finally blurt those magic words: "I'm going to!"

When I stand before God at the end of my life, I would hope that I would not have a single bit of talent left, and could say, I used everything you gave me.

—Erma Bombeck

But simply saying it doesn't make it so, and it sure doesn't make it easy. Here it is again: *you've got to step into the current so it can carry you.* You've got to plunge into the water of the writing life and learn to adjust to its twists and turns as you go along.

So let's make sure you really know what you're getting into here.

Still Crazy After All These Books

True commitment is a gift, a blessing, a burden, a curse, and sometimes it's all of those things at once. Just ask John Wesley Powell on the day he found out that two of his men, fellows who had abandoned the trip midway into it, had been subsequently killed by Indians. How did he feel about his commitment—and what it had asked of other people—then? Ask any of those retreat writers on any day when they were so discouraged and frightened about their fates that all they could do was sit in their rooms and stare out the window in despair. Ask any writer who's ever endured countless rejections or slogged through the bog in the middle of a novel. And ask the heroes of our world—the Nelson Mandelas, the Martin Luther Kings, the Susan B. Anthonys, and Nobel Peace Prize winners like Betty Williams and Mairead Corrigan—who have endured prison, death threats, ostracism, or assassination because of their incredible commitment to their cause.

Of course, some people might joke that writers need to *be* committed, rather than to have commitment, and sometimes we feel as if we can only agree with them. It's probably true that we're all at least a little bit crazy. But then, truly committed people usually look a little—or

I wrote for twelve years and collected 250 rejection slips before getting any fiction published, so I guess outside reinforcement isn't all that important to me.

—Lisa Alther

very—crazy to the outside world. If you don't look just a little bit nuts, you're probably not committed enough. Think how many people must have considered Nelson Mandela and Betty Williams to be crazy to risk their lives, and the lives of their families, in the cause of equality and peace. A lot of people certainly thought that men were crazy for trying to fly, or dive beneath the ocean, or land on the moon. And writers—like L. Frank Baum, whose *The Wonderful Wizard of Oz* was rejected dozens of times—who keep sending their manuscripts to publishers look like crazy fools to people who will be only too glad to tell them so.

No matter how big or soft or warm your bed is, you still have to get out of it.
—Grace Slick

Fortunately, not every commitment is huge or life-threatening. To get to the big commitments in our life, most of us have to start small. But every commitment we make, no matter how small it is, in any part of our life, strengthens our ability to make the kind of commitment we need to reach fulfillment on the writer's path.

Energy to Intention to Action

How can you tell if you're here? First comes the inner realization of having made a choice at last. "This *is* what I want. I want *this!*" You believe you can do it, and you feel convinced that you're going to do it. You feel elated, and that alone is enough to create energy to ride the wave of your intention all the way to action. You're really out there now, because in addition to the promise you make to yourself, you are announcing to the world that you are here and ready and going to accomplish something grand. Or if you aren't exactly announcing it, you are out of hiding and others get to see your efforts.

You're like a writer we know who wanted to become

a professional speaker but was afraid of humiliation. Everyone who knew him loved listening to his stories and encouraged him to give a presentation to some of the local groups to get started. He dragged his feet, but one day, without telling a soul, he put himself on the agenda of a small writers group and gave his first presentation. Just because he didn't announce it to anyone didn't mean that it wasn't a huge risk for him.

Talk about being vulnerable. It's one thing to make a decision in the quiet and privacy of your mind. It's quite another to tell someone else about it or to do a time line in your calendar or to make a date with a coauthor to begin outlining your project or, like the writer we mentioned, put something in writing and make it public, even if it's for your kid's school newspaper.

This business of learning how to commit came painfully to Lynn.

She's the first to admit that she wasn't always the kind of person who did what she said she would when she made a commitment, not as she is famous for now. She remembers those days when she would make small talk by saying to acquaintances, "We should get together sometime soon." And then one day, one of those people looked at Lynn and said, "Either take out your calendar or stop telling me that." Lynn was taken aback, caught in making a commitment she had no intention of keeping. That didn't fit with her ego's picture of herself at all, but it was the jolt she needed.

Lynn had to face whether or not she really wanted to have lunch with this woman. She did, so she took out her calendar and made a date. But more important, from that point on, Lynn thought more carefully about what commitment meant to her, in general. She stopped making commitments *of any size* if she had no intention of keeping them. And if she did intend to follow through with action, she knew that she was completely committed to it.

From that point on, every time she made a commitment that was followed by action, it built up her commitment muscles, until they were strong enough for an adventure that was her own personal voyage down the "Grand Canyon."

Lynn Puts Her Life Where Her Mouth Is

Which helps explain how, at age thirty, Lynn and her husband, Jerry, and their two toddlers and dog drove away from their life and traveled around the United States for twenty-three thousand miles in a van.

"When I was thirty," she recalls about that time in her life, "I suddenly found that I just couldn't bear the thought of living out the rest of my life according to somebody else's plan. Up to that time, I had followed all the rules, although I had no idea whose rules I was following. Someone called Conventional Wisdom, perhaps? I had the education, the husband, the kid, the house, the second kid, and now the pressure was starting to build for the bigger house, preferably in the suburbs. At this rate, I thought I might as well die, because I felt as if the end of my story were already written for me, and that I wasn't really needed to live it out.

"So I did the only thing that made sense to me. . . . I said yes to my husband's wild suggestion that we travel through Central and South America . . . sort of. The more we talked about the idea, the more my practical side took over. Since we didn't speak a word of Spanish

"Now" is the operative word. Everything you've put in your way is just a method of putting off the hour when you could actually be doing your dream.

—Barbara Sher

and were traveling with toddlers who might get sick, I thought we should travel where we at least spoke the language. But the part of me that made a commitment to change suggested we use the trip to find a new place to live along with a new life. And to make sure there was no turning back, we decided to sell everything we owned, including our house and all our possessions."

Once they made the commitment and set things in motion, they chose their route, a whimsical and charming one: they decided to follow the changing leaves of autumn.

"Seven months later, we ended up in California, the one place we both swore we'd never live, making our new life there."

To paraphrase Professor Higgins in *My Fair Lady*, "By George, they did it."

Jack London did it, too, when he vowed to travel around the world, with no more knowledge of where he was going than Lynn and her family had when they set out. "Only one thing is definite," he wrote in *The Cruise of the Snark* in 1919, "and that is that our first port of call will be Honolulu. We shall make up our minds as we get nearer. In a general way we know that we shall wander through the South Seas, take in Samoa . . . after that the voyage becomes too vague to describe."

It's never too late to be what you might have been.
—George Eliot

For Nancy on the fateful day when she knew she wanted to write fiction full-time, taking the action step of commitment meant going home to ask her husband, "How would you feel if I didn't make any money for a long time?" Then it meant calling all of her freelance clients that very day and giving them thirty days' notice.

It will mean different things for you than it does for anybody else. But like Nancy or Lynn or John Wesley

Powell or thirty writers in Kentucky, if you're truly "committed," you will need to do something external—something in the real world—to prove it and to anchor your decision.

Speaking your commitment out loud is extremely important.

If you're like Lynn, you might break promises to yourself, but once you've made a date with someone else, you *will* show up and keep your commitment. (While we were writing this book, Nancy often said to other people, "I'm not worried about getting it done. *Lynn* never misses deadlines!") When Nancy decided to try to get a mystery novel written and published, "I told everybody I knew that I was working on a novel, because that way I'd feel completely humiliated in front of everybody if I failed. I wanted to raise the stakes as high as possible to make it harder for me to back down."

The important thing about anchoring your inner commitment to the real world is that you make it visible to yourself and to other people in some way. It will inform you and them that you mean it, you're serious this time. It will raise the stakes for you and make it harder for you to ignore that epiphany, that inner moment of yes. It will make the invisible visible. By taking an action in the real world, you will move past yes and on to "yes, and . . ."

Writer after writer has described writing to us in the same way that Nancy and Lynn and explorers like Jack London have described their adventures—as something they felt compelled, even called, to do, and that they committed to it without a contract or a deadline in sight and often with only the barest notion of an idea of where their writing, or their voyage, was headed.

> *The measure of achievement is not winning awards. It's doing something that you appreciate, something you believe is worthwhile. I think of my strawberry soufflé. I did that at least twenty-eight times before I finally conquered it.*
> —Julia Child

Learn as You Go

*I've arrived at
this outermost
edge of my life by
my own actions.
Where I am is
thoroughly
unacceptable.
Therefore, I must
stop doing what
I've been doing.*

—Alice Koller

For many authors, the art of writing is something they learn as they go, and they may publish many books before they ever feel confident about their skills. In spite of those insecurities, they commit to writing—again and again—in much the same way Jack London chose his boat: "The ketch retains the cruising virtues of the yawl. . . . The foregoing must be taken with a grain of salt. It is all theory in my head. I've never sailed a ketch, nor even seen one. . . . Wait til I get out on the ocean, then I'll be able to tell more about the cruising and sailing qualities of the ketch."

Can you *believe* that? He took off on the deep blue sea in a kind of boat he'd never even been on, much less ever sailed! He sort of had an itinerary. He kind of knew how long he'd be gone. But he so wanted to do this crazy thing that he made the commitment. He was willing to cast off and to learn as he went, even if he died trying: "Neither Roscoe nor I knows anything about navigation, and the summer is gone, and we are about to start, and the problems are thicker than ever, and the treasury is stuffed with emptiness. Well, anyway, it takes years to learn seamanship, and both of us are seamen. If we don't find the time, we'll lay in the books and instruments and teach ourselves navigation on the ocean between San Francisco and Hawaii."

Amazing. And so similar to how many writers get started:

"I don't know anything about publishing," they might say, "and my checking account is stuffed with emptiness. Well, anyway, it takes years to become a good novelist. I'll lay in books and notepads and teach myself how to write during my coffee breaks."

That's what Don Coldsmith did—he is a full-time Western writer now with many books to his credit—but once he was a doctor who sat and wrote in the hallways of the Emporia, Kansas, hospital where he practiced medicine. One of the nurses remembers it well. "I remember seeing Don in between operations," she told Nancy. "There he'd be in his hospital greens, just sitting in the corridor, writing in a notebook."

Scott Turow wrote his first book on the commuter trains of Chicago as he traveled to and from his law office. Both of those men committed—to what, they hardly knew—and then they set sail, learning in the process of doing.

Jack London pulled it off—and lived to write *The Cruise of the Snark*.

Lynn and her family pulled it off, and she lived to tell us about it.

By making such a huge commitment and following through with it completely, Lynn gave herself a lot of insights, as every committed adventurer—and writer—does. The first of her insights was about time. "Pretrip, I lived on a treadmill," she says. "I got up each morning, hopped on the treadmill, ran as fast as I could, and fell into bed exhausted each night. It never occurred to me there was any other way to do it.

"But time took on a new meaning on the trip. There was a rhythm to travel that I had never experienced before. I soon realized that if I didn't enjoy the moment I was in, it would be miles behind me before long, and I'd never have the same experience or opportunity again. So I learned to live in the present and appreciate it for what it had to offer. That may sound simplistic to people who already know that, but I had never realized before the trip just how much of my time I spent thinking about

What you don't do can be a destructive force.
—Eleanor Roosevelt

the past or planning for the future and missing the moments in front of my nose."

Her second big aha was that she had one life to live—or at least, she'd only live this life once—and that she was in charge of it.

"I know that probably sounds elementary to a lot of people," she says, "but it was a dramatic revelation for me at the time. I finally got it, that if I wasted time, I'd never have it again. I needed to get clear on what my goals and priorities were so I could structure my life to meet them instead of merely react to life as it came my way. Because I made that dramatic commitment, I learned that I was in charge of my life."

The Shuttered Lantern

Now, when she thinks of the word *commitment*, Lynn pictures a shuttered lantern with light glowing around the edges of the shutters.

"Most people live their whole lives as if they were shuttered lanterns," she says, from the vantage point of her thirty years as a therapist. "They search all their life long to find something else, or somebody else, to light their path for them, not realizing that all the light they'll ever need is there inside themselves. They're scared to lift the shutter, or maybe they don't even know there's a latch to unfasten. And so they stumble along in the dark, trying to find their way with the little bit of their own light that trickles out at the edges or with the reflected light of someone else. That's what it's like to live with the shutters down. That's what it's like to live without committing yourself to something fully and with passion."

Most of the commitments that writers make are far

Keep doing what you're doing and you'll keep getting what you're getting.

—Anonymous

less dramatic than changing their whole lives. But even the smallest commitment, made wholeheartedly, feels clean, clear, energizing. Commitment feels great, even when there's a part of you that's still scared to death, as is often true for writers who make any of the following commitments to their craft: sending a check to register for a writers conference, sitting down with a timer and writing for a half hour a day, writing five pages, plunking down the credit card to pay for a new laptop, sending out a manuscript to an agent or editor, showing up at a writers group, doing the rewrites, calling an editor. In each of those cases, a realization is followed by a decision and then by an action. And as you do it, it's normal to feel relieved and scared and nervous and dedicated and proud and shaky all at the same time.

Commitments can happen in a flash. One minute, you're blind; the next minute, you can see. It happened just that way to Nancy on the day she made the amazing commitment to leave all of her freelance clients and become a full-time fiction writer, before she'd ever written a novel or sold a single short story.

"It was 1981," Nancy reflected, "and I had been a freelance commercial writer for about eight years and was growing increasingly unhappy with it. One day, I had lunch with a friend. I was complaining to her about how much I hated what I was doing for a living and how all I really wanted to do was write mystery novels for the rest of my life. I'd only ever written about forty pages of one, you understand, but that's how I felt, more passionately than I'd ever felt anything before.

"Out of the blue, my friend blurted, 'You know what's wrong with you? You're just afraid to do it.'

"Afraid? Me? The lightbulb over my head switched on. She was right. It was so obvious. It was so true. I was afraid to stop doing what I hated to do, and I was afraid to start doing what I longed to do. I remember a very clear moment then of sitting at the table with her and thinking to myself that I had a choice in this moment, and that it was an important one that could affect the rest of my life. I could choose to fall back into my fears and the status quo, or I could choose to make a commitment to move forward. I thought about what it was like to ski, about how you have to go against all of your instincts and lean down the mountain, even though you feel sure you're going to fall, but that's the only way you'll ever learn to ski. In that moment, I reflected back on my skiing. I realized I had to lean down the mountain of my life, despite my fears, or I'd never make my dreams come true.

" 'I'll do it,' I said to my friend. Just like that. That's literally how fast it happened; that's how the rest of my life began. It was a eureka moment. My whole life changed in an instant, because I had a realization, I made a decision, and I took the action of telling her my intention. There would be a few more actions to come, to nail this step down, but those were for later."

Commitment + Great Risk = Huge Rewards

But what if commitment plus risk ends in failure? Nancy announces she's going to write fiction and then doesn't do it or never sells anything? The new company folds, the book never gets published, Lynn and her family run out of gas. Is it worth it then? We can't presume to say. We can only say that we ensure failure by not committing and that every time we've risked something and failed, we've also learned something important along the way. For us, that makes commitment essential for success and worthwhile even in failure. But you know yourself better than we do, and only you can make that determination for yourself.

We can tell you this, however: most published writers say that if they'd realized when they started how hard it is to get published, how poor the odds, how stiff the winds against them, they might have quailed and lowered their sails, and never tried to write at all. It's too hard, they would have thought; it's too scary. The publishing sea is too big, and my writing boat is too small. Fortunately, just like Jack London, most writers who eventually get published are blissfully ignorant of all that, and so they—we, you—just crazily commit to starting . . . and then we start.

We're not suggesting that you act recklessly to prove your commitment to writing. You don't have to set out blindly. But we are saying that you can't "sail" if you're not committed to doing it. If you do make the commitment, then it's possible that if you show up at the dock dressed in navy blues, if you step into the boat and push off from the shore and row, however poorly, you might just ride the current to the other shore. Eventually, with practice and very sore shoulders, the rowing will come easier. You may even learn to navigate by the stars. Or possibly not. But if you've been paying attention to the gist of this step, one thing is sure: if you never step into the current, it can never carry you.

According to Lawrence Durrell, "It doesn't matter whether you're first rate, second rate, or third rate, but it's of vital importance that the water finds its own level and that you do the very best you can with the powers that are given you." He called it "utterly immoral to be slothful about the qualities you have." If that sounds too brutally moralistic, then let's just say that profound commitment feels profoundly good. It sure beats depression.

There is a need to find and sing our own song, to stretch our limbs and shake them in a dance so wild that nothing can roost there, that stirs the yearning for solitary voyage.

—Barbara
Lazear Ascher

But—and here's the rub of failure again—what if not-writing has been hard for you, but writing looks as if it may be hard, too? (And we can tell you, it will be.) What if it would mean you'll have to make scary changes in your life? You'll have to take time you don't have. You'll have to face failure and rejection. You'll have to make somebody unhappy. You might go broke. You're already broke. You'll have to make sacrifices or ask them of other people. You're too old. You're too young. You'd lose your pension. You'd lose your insurance. You'd have to put your own interests first. You'd have to . . . and so on.

Well, as Mae West said, "When choosing between two evils, I always like to choose the one I've never done before." So if you've already tried *not* writing . . . or not writing what you want to write . . . or not writing as much as you want . . . or not writing up to the quality you want, then why not make the commitment to another choice this time? If you've already tried *not* writing, and that hurt, can writing possibly hurt more?

If you never write, you can never be a writer.

If you never write something different, you can never get out of the rut you may be in.

If you never write more, you can never produce more.

If you never submit anything, you can never publish it.

But if you *do* show up at your computer or notebook, if you start somewhere, by putting down words just like a writer, then you just might end up being a writer.

Or will you?

"The Whole Trouble with You Is . . ."

Has anyone ever told you, "You know, the whole trouble with you is, you're just one of those people who can't commit"? That's what Nancy's boss told her more than thirty years ago.

"When I was twenty-two years old and fresh out of journalism school, I took a job at a small local newspaper," she remembers. "About a year into it, my publisher said to me, 'Nancy, when are you ever going to commit yourself to something?' I felt a little shocked to hear him say it, but it didn't hurt my feelings, because I knew it was true. I stood outside of everything. Very little engaged me emotionally. I didn't have a sense of passion about anything, really, and as a consequence, I didn't have much confidence, either.

"One of the ways that I've always been able to tell if I was committed to something was by looking at other people who were involved in the same thing. For instance, at that newspaper, my best friend was a woman of my own age, Susan White, who is now a journalist in San Diego. I could look at Susan and see the difference between us. She was fascinated by the stories we covered, and she really cared about the people in them. I think that's why she was so passionate and committed— because she loved her job."

After "flunking" journalism, Nancy turned to writing training programs for a corporation, but once again, she felt like an outsider watching other people who were committed to their careers. The same thing happened when she became a commercial freelance writer. It wasn't until many years had passed that she found something that engaged her interest so passionately—writing fiction—

Swing hard, in case they throw the ball while you're swinging.

—Duke Snider

that she simply had to do it. By that time, she was thirty-five years old, but, as she said, "I felt as if my life were only then getting started. In hindsight, I realize that an interest in fiction probably shouldn't have surprised me as much as it did at the time. I had always loved to read novels, after all, especially mysteries. And so the day finally came when I found what I really wanted to do. Once I found that, commitment just seemed to follow."

Do you think *you* have a commitment problem?

Creatures of Conventional Wisdom

We'll venture to say that what might be happening is that you're simply not doing what you want to do. You might have become a creature of conventional wisdom and got so good at following it, you don't realize you have choices.

How does one become a creature of conventional wisdom? We live in a society that claims to encourage diversity, but deep down inside, most people seem to believe there is only one way to do things, right down to how often you should make your bed (once a day, in the morning) to how many glasses of water you should drink (eight glasses a day) to how much television you should watch (three hours, max). It's a funny form of competition, really. "Don't you drink any more water than that?" "I was over at Marge's house yesterday afternoon, and do you know, her beds weren't even made!" "They let that child watch way too much television."

While it's true that everyone wants to belong and everyone wants to feel significant, that often means doing things the way everybody else does them. And yet Lynn can testify, from years of watching clients in

Sarah Ban Breathnach was rejected thirty-one times before Warner Books bought Simple Abundance.

therapy, that when all those *one right ways* come in the window, that's when commitment and focus fly out.

Case in point. Take the kid who supposedly can't commit or focus. The proof? Homework forgotten, jacket lost, teeth unbrushed, clothes wrinkled and lying on the floor, drum set forgotten in the corner. Nothing happens without reminders and nagging. And we all know that it's only kids who are like this, right?

So we give the kid a label and sometimes a pill and neglect the rest of the evidence that clearly proves that he isn't flawed, just disinterested. The proof? Three hundred hours spent zeroed in on the computer game to reach the next level, snowboard magazines organized by date and year on the shelf, CDs alphabetized, baseball stats for the last fifty years rolling off the tip of the tongue, practicing a new guitar riff while jumping off the bed looking like a rock star for hours on end. When he wants to, that kid can commit and focus like a laser beam. He's just not interested in the other stuff. And c'mon, let's be honest—how fascinating do *you* find it to clean your room and do your homework?

"But we have to do those things," you say?

To put this bluntly—a lot of people who are devoted to their writing do not make their beds every day, if ever. They didn't make straight A's or even straight B's. Some even made straight F's. When they're immersed in their writing, they may have the world's worst diet—all coffee, sugar, and starches. And there are times when they've written so much and so hard that their brain feels as if they'd stuck the vacuum cleaner hose up to one ear and sucked it all out, and all they are capable of doing then is staring dumbly for hours on end at a television set or a movie screen. As for their physical appearance, let's not even bring that up. Certain things should never be

If you have a dream of writing, that's wishful thinking. If you have a commitment to writing, that's the way to make dreams come true.

—Nancy Pickard

spoken aloud in public, mainly because our friends would kill us. Well, all right, if you twist our arms, we'll tell you one story:

We know a best-selling romance novelist, a beautiful woman, whose husband once said to her, "No offense, honey, but I can always tell how far along you are in a book by your appearance." Do you think it was the sweatpants she'd worn for a week? The makeup she hadn't put on since Christmas? Or was it her stringy hair? "This is one advantage," Nancy says to Lynn, "that we single writers may have over you married ones. At least there's nobody to gross out."

Oh, sure, some writers are better at leading consistently healthy lifestyles than others are. Lynn's good at it. She walks, works out, eats nutritious meals that she plans and cooks, and always looks terrific, to hear her husband tell it. (To be fair, it must also be reported—by Nancy—that this is a saint of a husband who makes the beds, cleans the condo, and runs their errands and finances.)

When Nancy, on the other hand, is deep into a novel, her bed goes unmade for weeks on end. And don't even ask about the dusting, OK? (True story: Once on an airplane, a woman sat down next to a friend of Nancy's who was reading a Jenny Cain mystery. "Oh, I was in her house one time," the woman said to Nancy's friend, with a gesture toward the book jacket. "I saw dust balls under her couch." Nancy doesn't think it's true about the woman's having been in her house, but then how did she know about the dust balls?) She is all too aware that she needs stamina and physical well-being, the kind that comes from being a runner, say, and from eating smart. She tends to think about that as she's standing in front of the refrigerator nibbling cold quiche while her third pot of coffee is perking.

The point is that writers give up a lot of "doing things the one right way" in order to commit themselves to what they want to do—that is, write. And thank God they do, or we wouldn't have books to read or magazines to enjoy or poems to share or plays to attend or any other kind of pleasure that derives from the written word. Which would you rather, that J. K. Rowling stayed home and cleaned house or that she went to that coffee shop and wrote about Harry Potter?

The minute you start doing mostly or only what you think you should, you squeeze out of your life the things you want to do, as if all that damned conventional wisdom were a wringer and your life were a wet mop. The minute you stop doing what you want to do, you lose interest and then focus and then commitment. It's a vicious circle that starts with "I have to," comes around to "I forgot to," and sadly ends up with "I don't know what's wrong with me."

You're as bored as a kid with a room to clean, that's what's wrong with you.

If you aren't focused on anything you like, if you think you have no passion, if you don't feel deeply committed to much of anything, maybe that's because you aren't interested in much of anything you're doing. Like those kids with worried parents, you don't suffer from a character flaw, you don't have a disease, you don't need a pill, and you don't need to be labeled. Maybe all you need to do is what you really want to do, if you can figure out a way. If you need to, you can always wrap that conventional wisdom up in a box and put in on a shelf, just in case you want it back someday. *Then* you'll feel

Who in their right mind would say, "I am committed to being a failed writer. I will go all out to be mediocre"?
—Nancy Pickard

the focus; then you'll have the passion and commitment that's been missing from your life, maybe even all of your life.

Judy Goldman, author of *The Slow Way Back*, told us, "I kept waiting for someone to tell me, 'Don't do so many errands. Don't be such a good mother and wife. Don't run such an efficient household.' But no one in the world was ever going to tell me that! I had to learn to be a medium mother and wife, to run a semiefficient household. I had to put writing at the top of my list and the drugstore and dry cleaner's at the bottom. That's the real secret: we think that if we run all our errands, then we can sit down and write. That's wrong. First, we get our writing in. Then we tackle the to-do list."

"I Don't Do Schedules," Says M. Black and White

A lot of people use the excuse of not having enough time to write, and they are correct, but not because there aren't enough hours in the day but because they refuse to schedule their time. It's amazing how hard they fight "routines," when clearly, they live an unrewarding routine every day of their lives—the routine of doing nothing with intention. And commitment is about nothing if it's not about intention.

Committing to your writing isn't an all-or-nothing affair for many writers. Take Judith Greber, aka Gillian Roberts. She said, "Somebody famous—was it Sartre?— said that a person could either live or write. I understand what he meant, but I can't bear the idea. I want both. Therefore, I handle those times by arranging for as much unbroken time as works with the rest of my life. But only that much. I still break in order to visit with or en-

There are no little events in life, those we think of no consequence may be full of fate, and it is at our own risk if we neglect the acquaintances and opportunities that seem to be casually offered and of small importance.

—Amelia Barr

tertain friends, to travel and enjoy the benefits of the City (that's what northern Californians call San Francisco) and area's offerings, and of course, to spend time with my family." Her intention is not only for writing but also for balance. She's fully committed to both, which is why she gets them, even though it's not always easy.

Lynn is a lot like Judy in that she enjoys a certain amount of balance in her life and knows how to create it. When she started her writing career, at least the serious part of it, she set aside weekends to write. Soon, she found out that writing had become a much larger part of her life than it used to be, so she had to think through her schedule and figure out how she could write without "killing" herself.

One way she practices commitment to living the writing life is to be proactive, planning ahead instead of responding to a problem. At the time when she realized she wanted to write more often, she took out her calendar and saw that with a bit of reshuffling, she could free up mornings for writing. Then she decided that writing on weekends was also fine as long as at least one day was set aside for skiing or hiking or exploring. And on the writing days, she'd stop by 3:00 P.M. to enjoy other activities.

To handle the chaos of working on multiple projects at once, she set up the "bag-method filing system." She has plastic bags, cloth bags, wicker bags, and paper bags where she places scraps of paper with ideas as they come up. Then, when she has time to work on a project, she can grab the appropriate bag instead of wasting time sorting through piles of papers.

"Once I've signed a contract, I'm a big scheduler," Lynn says. "I take out my calendar and write in dates when I can go away for anywhere from a four-day weekend to a two-week vacation to write. [Lynn's favorite vacation is a writing vacation, in which she goes somewhere beautiful and spends mornings at the computer and afternoons exploring and playing.] I prefer writing with other people, so this requires some real shuffling to get two busy schedules to coincide. We start at the deadline and work our way backward to make sure we have scheduled the time needed to complete our project.

What had seemed easy in imagination was rather hard in reality.

—L. M. Montgomery

"I can't stress enough that for me, commitment involves a lot of planning and scheduling so that I have the time available to write. My writing isn't a haphazard occurrence but much more a thought-out practice. Sometimes, I wish I had more time to write, but deep down, I believe that I'm lucky because I don't have all the time in the world. It helps me cherish and use what time I have. And I'm ever so fortunate that my day job is working with people, so I can continually test out my ideas and share what I'm learning with them. I think the combination helps me stay honest about what works and what doesn't. Everything gets field-tested almost as quickly as I create it."

Once Upon a Time, You Knew What You Wanted Most

Maybe if you take a little time to pull out your calendar or think through how you currently spend your time, you might find a window of time to write or more time to write. But if you are still struggling with trying to want something enough to commit to it, we suggest that you take a trip back to your diaries or baby books or childhood memories. They can help you rediscover that place where you have always known what you wanted to be and do.

Lynn has memories of wanting to be Davy Crockett or Sacagawea. Now people call her a trailblazer, a pathfinder, a pioneer, for the ways in which she conducts therapy and for the material she puts in her books. When Nancy was ten years old, she wrote, "When I grow up, I will be perfectly happy if I can have horses, solve mysteries, be happily married, and help people." Thirty years later, she was a mystery writer, married to a rancher, and trying to help new writers get published.

What do you remember about what you used to want?

Allow yourself to travel back to a time before the conventional wisdom took over and made you settle for less than you wanted for yourself. What were your dreams for yourself? What fascinated you? What did you love to do? When you daydreamed, what were those fantasies about? What did you want to be when you grew up? That's where you'll find clues to what you want to do now and what you want to write now.

Jack London knew the answer a century ago.

He wrote in *The Cruise of the Snark*, "When philosophy has maundered ponderously for a month, telling the individual what he must do, the individual says, in an instant, 'I like,' and does something else, and philosophy goes glimmering." He said, "The things I like constitute my set of values. The thing I like most of all is personal achievement—not achievement for the world's applause, but achievement for my own delight. It is the old 'I did it! I did it! With my own hands I did it!'"

Total commitment comes from feeling tremendously interested in something and leads to total involvement. Commitment in moderation comes from moderate

The hard part for me was to admit that I wanted to write. If I didn't admit that fact, I didn't have to worry about being disappointed about failing. Just to think, "I want to be a writer," scared me. It was even scarier to say, "I want to be a writer."

—Cecil Murphey

interest and leads to moderate involvement. Sporadic or halfhearted commitment comes from halfhearted interest and produces intermittent and halfhearted involvement, and so on. We reap involvement in exact proportion to the commitment we sow, and we are committed to the precise extent that we feel interest or that we *allow* ourselves to feel it. Sadly, a whole lot of people already know what interests them, but for reasons of their own, they won't—or can't—allow themselves to feel it.

Sue Grafton's Five-Step Commitment Checklist

1. *What do I want?*
2. *Where am I in the process?*
3. *How can I make room in my life for this change?*
4. *What's standing in my way?*
5. *What is the next step?*

What's your level of interest in writing? How deeply do you feel it? How much commitment do you have to it? How involved are you in it? These are not meant to be judgmental questions; we're just asking. We're just collecting information. Or, rather, you are. You're the only one who'll hear your answers, unless you choose to share them with somebody else. So what would you say? How would you rate your commitment to what you're writing (or not writing)? Full? Partial? Wholehearted? Halfhearted? Fainthearted? Hesitant? Reluctant? Nonexistent? If "most committed" is a tiger in pursuit of a wildebeest and "least committed" is a sleeping lion, then where on the scale of wild things are you?

Some of Lynn's friends liken her to a jet plane, "because by the time you hear the noise, the jet is already miles away." Her commitment is like the tiger in pursuit when it's time to put a book project together. She's a doer, and everyone who knows her knows that about her. She even calls herself a "do, do" therapist (pun intended), "because my goal is to get my clients talking less and doing more. I take commitment seriously and won't stop until a project is under way."

Lynn's motto is, "If you mean it, say it, and if you say it, do it. Otherwise, keep your mouth shut and listen."

Born to Write

Some writers say they've always known that writing was what they were meant to do. It's as if they were born already "committed" to it. One suspects that may have been true of someone like the late humorist James Thurber, who said, "I never quite know when I'm not writing. Sometimes my wife comes up to me at a party and says, 'Dammit, Thurber, stop writing.' She usually catches me in the middle of a paragraph. Or my daughter will look up from the dinner table and ask, 'Is he sick?' 'No,' my wife says, 'he's writing something.' "

Do you wish you were that involved in your writing? How involved *do* you want to be, really? How much of your life do you honestly want it to consume? Whatever your true answer, then that's exactly how much commitment you'll have with which to launch your hopes and dreams. If you want to shoot for a column in your local suburban newspaper, maybe you'll only need a few gallons of low-octane fuel, but if you're aiming for the moon of international best-seller-dom, you'd better strap on hydrogen and more.

We know it seems as if some writers are just born with booster rockets attached to their backsides. You'd think they came out of the womb with a pen in their fist. They wrote a poem by age three, a short story in kindergarten, a novel in sixth grade. We hate them, don't we? Most of us aren't like that at all. We don't feel born to write what we end up writing—at least, not until we start doing it. And it can take a long, hard time to get there. For Nancy, the process of reaching a point of passionate commitment took thirty-five years.

But what if commitment comes even harder for you than it did for her?

Patience Is Not My Middle Name

To go against the dominant thinking of your friends, of most of the people you see every day, is perhaps the most difficult act of heroism you can perform.

—Theodore H. White

Sometimes, we commit to writing, or to a writing project, because the thought of doing it fills our hearts with joy or eagerness. But many writers/people find it very hard to figure out what they want, much less acknowledge it, feel it, commit to it, and go after it. It seems to them as if passion and commitment are special gifts that are reserved for other people and never for them. They may feel perpetually underprivileged or deprived; they may feel perplexed and resentful, or like outsiders in the game of life. They think they want to play, they see other people playing hard and enthusiastically, but somehow it all escapes them. They feel as if they've stood forever on the sidelines. They just can't seem to work up enough interest to care that much, to risk that much, to work that hard, to throw themselves bodily into . . . anything.

What's going on in cases like that?

If you suffer from an inability to commit, maybe you're like Nancy, who apparently needed to live long enough to attain the level of maturity and experience to allow her to find, express, and then do what she passionately wanted to do. As an optimist once said, "The world is full of magical things just waiting for our wits to grow sharper." Maybe it's no accident that the majority of mystery writers start their careers in middle age; maybe their wits have to grow sharp enough to create those puzzles.

Sometimes, it's "just" a matter of cosmic timing.

After all, the stars do need to line up for you to be able to write and/or get published: you have to be ready, but so does your environment and so do the other people involved. You may have the Great American Novel all written, for instance, but if New York isn't ready to recognize its worth, then the time's not right. Like L. Frank Baum, the author of *Wonderful Wizard of Oz*, who sent his book out more than forty times, you may have to wait a long time. Or maybe you've got your home and your family all set up to support your writing endeavors, but the only problem is that you yourself are as blocked as Hoover Dam. Again, the cosmic timing's off. Or maybe you're writing well, and there's an editor out there who would love to buy your historical novel, but the market for that kind of book—your "environment"—is not co-operating right now.

Sometimes, there's no way to know if a timing problem is at the root of your commitment deprivation. But if nothing's happening, if you feel as if you're waiting for your life to start, then there's something very important that you need to know: *waiting is an art in itself.*

Waiting doesn't mean giving up and letting fate take its course. That's a negative attitude. And don't get confused, thinking that "waiting for fate" is the same thing as "going with the flow." Waiting for fate is like sitting on a riverbank watching your own life flow past you. "Oh, look, there goes my career. Bye-bye." "Here comes a tree caught in the river, and I think it's going to hit me. Ouch." "Hey, will you look at that? Here comes my marriage . . . Oops, there it goes." Going with the flow, by contrast (and yes, we must repeat ourselves once again to underline this extremely important point), means plunging into the water of life and learning to adjust to its twists and turns as you—and it—surge along. Going with the flow is an activity; waiting for fate is a passivity.

Waiting means not pushing at the wrong time, because that can get you into danger. Yes, maybe if you push hard enough, you can annoy that agent into looking at your proposal, but maybe she's not the right agent

Learn to say no. It will be of more use to you than to be able to read Latin.

—Charles Haddon Spurgeon

for you. Maybe if you accepted that fact and used your time of waiting constructively, maybe eventually you'd find a better agent for you. Or maybe that agent you pushed will take you on as a client but will never try hard for you, because you pushed too hard when you should have backed off.

It's hard to know; harder for some people than for others.

Waiting *does* mean accepting how things are for now, but acceptance is in no way the same as resignation. Acceptance brings peace; resignation brings depression. If, instead of waiting actively, you find yourself slumped in a chair morosely staring out your window for hours on end, that's depression, a dangerous state. It's certainly a flashing red light warning of flagging commitment.

The art of waiting is, we cannot emphasize enough, an *active* art, not a passive one. It's a behavior. It's the art of actively keeping a positive attitude, which can require a great deal of self-discipline and effort, and it's the art of using the time while you wait for self-examination and self-improvement. There are skills you can learn. There is information you can gather. There is introspection to be done, always remembering Ralph Waldo Emerson's wisest admonition of all: "An unexamined life is not worth living." In that regard, waiting will certainly bring you many opportunities to build your character.

Sometimes, we just have to wait . . . and wait . . . and wait.

Nina Osier echoes that in her advice to writers: "When I wanted to be published most desperately was after I'd starting writing again when I was past forty. I started getting the 'good rejections' almost immediately. What was it like? Frustrating, of course! But by now, I

Don't be afraid your life will end; be afraid it will never begin.
—Grace Hansen

was going to keep doing this anyway, and I was too old to care what anyone else thought of the time I was devoting to it. My mantra became, 'It's my life. I'd rather do this and fail at it than do anything else in the world.' I'd tell authors, do it for yourself because it gives you great joy, or for heaven's sake, don't bother!"

How we "behave" during that difficult time may determine how ready we are to respond successfully to our "fate" when it takes a turn for the better.

What good will it do if the market changes and readers are clamoring for historicals and you haven't kept up with your research?

What good will it do you if there's an editor who would love your stuff but you don't have anything ready to show her?

What good will it do if you could finally come unblocked but your skills are so rusty you get blocked all over again?

What good will it do if you've allowed yourself to become so demoralized by the waiting that when the stars shift, you're in a total eclipse of the psyche?

Sometimes, it all depends on *how* you wait.

> *Growth itself contains the germ of happiness.*
> —Pearl
> S. Buck

We Warned You, Writing Is Hard

A lot of people talk a good writing game. They'll tell you that they're writers or they want to write or someday they're going to write. But are they *writing*? Will "someday" ever come? Are those two tongues we talked about in Wanting in alignment? Is that tongue in the shoe agreeing with the one in their mouth? There's a *reason* that it takes a whole lot of passion and commitment to become the writer you've always wanted to be. And that reason is that writing anything beyond easy little personal ditties involves hard work, and not everybody's willing to take that on. And if you don't believe us, take it from these authors.

"Successful people are the ones who are willing to do what other people don't want to do," said Donald Riggs.

Sue Grafton, author of the Kinsey Millhone alphabet mysteries, says, "Go all out. Failure is so easy. Success forces others to look at their lives. You never know where it will take you."

Linda Barnes, author of *Steel Guitar*, says, "You can't steal second with your foot on first."

Jeffrey Marks, author of *The Ambush of My Name*, says, "Commitment is putting the first word to paper. . . ."

Dan Eckstein, author of hundreds of journal articles and several books on Adlerian therapy, says, "Commitment, hmmm, let's see. Right now I am over deadline by two months on two books. My commitment is to birth those projects, even though they have been in the womb too long. And my commitment is to quality. So that leaves me balancing two conflicting commitments—my agreement to meet a deadline and my need for perfection. Not to mention my commitment to mentoring, which is why I'm taking time from my writing to answer this question, thus furthering the imbalance in my life because I am ignoring my commitment to physical exercise and, instead, writing all hours of the night."

So Dan Eckstein writes all night. Most people wouldn't do that. Remember, we told in an earlier chapter how best-selling romance author Julie Garwood used to get up and start writing every morning before she made breakfast for her husband and three children? Most people would roll over and go back to sleep. And we told how mystery writer Martha Powers used to kiss her children good night and then write until four in the morning? Most people would think that's nuts.

Don't kid yourself, and we won't try to kid you, either. Writing can be very hard. Getting the time to write can seem nearly impossible. Having enough energy when you *do* find the time may seem like a pipe dream. And yet writers write. When it's hard. When they don't have the time. When they're tired. They write. That's what writers do. They write. That's how you can tell they're writers. The tongue in their mouths ("I want to write") matches the tongue in their shoes ("I walk over to my computer, sit down, and write").

In the long run, men hit only what they aim at.
—Henry David Thoreau

And It Takes a Long Time

Maybe you've heard it said that it takes about ten years to become truly good at anything. That's as true of writing as it is of anything else. If you want to write anything beyond occasional entries in your journal, if you want to be a good writer, if you want to find an audience for your work, then when you commit yourself to writing, you're committing yourself to the long haul. We think that it's well for you to know this and that we'd be doing you a disservice if we tried to make writing look easier than it really is.

But maybe your writing goals aren't very serious right now. Maybe you'd be thrilled just to pen a poem you could read to your grandchildren. Maybe you'd be really happy to write one short story this year and another one next year. Maybe you only want to write now and then for your own delight. Maybe you couldn't care less if you ever get published. We find that hard to believe—it would make you as rare as certain species of tree frog—but if you say so, we'll accept that. But you know what? It doesn't matter how modest or lofty your writing goals. However humble, they still need the fuel of commitment to launch them, fly them, and land them successfully.

It almost sounds as if this is the end of the trail, doesn't it? We've rolled through unhappiness, wanting, and now commitment. We're already talking about taking action, doing it, writing, becoming successful, and it sounds as if you're really on your way. But that's not how this path works.

Just when you get your commitment off the ground . . .

You may find your wings starting to wobble, your boat going under, your words faltering, your heart quailing. That's the good news, because it means you're moving along into Wavering, the fourth step on the writer's path.

Wavering

Step Four on the Writer's Path

· ·

> *First writer (at a cocktail party): "I'm working on my new novel."*
> *Second writer: "Neither am I."*
>
> —Cartoon caption in *Private Eye*

> *Writer's block is going to happen to you. You will read what little you've written lately and see with absolute clarity that it is total dog shit.*
>
> —Anne Lamott, *Bird by Bird*

Well, it had seemed like a good idea at the time. When writer Michael Bane strapped on his scuba gear, the prospect of diving into the underwater labyrinth of caverns in north central Florida sounded thrilling. It's a dark, cool, fascinating world down there, and he was determined to see it, even if that meant following a lifeline and a flashlight deep under the earth and water.

Michael really wanted this dive, and he wanted to write about it for a book he was doing about a "regular guy's" adventures in extreme sports. Cave diving was about as extreme as it got. A top instructor had warned Mike that he'd be plunging into "the most unforgiving environment on earth," where one mistake could kill him, and do so most unpleasantly.

But Michael's desire was strong enough to fuel an equally strong commitment. Despite some early trepidation, he had fulfilled the tough prerequisites that his guides demanded of him—a minimum of fifteen cave dives into at least five different caves, and that was on top of the other scuba courses he took just to reach this last stage of certification.

To think too long about doing a thing often becomes its undoing.

—Eva Young

But here he was at last, staring at the reality of his goal—a starry night, a dark lake, and a small underwater entrance to the labyrinth—and he was seized with a primitive fear of small, dark places. Of suffocating. Of drowning. Of getting lost. He imagined himself squeezing through tunnels so narrow his tanks would scrape against the walls. Tons of water and earth would surround him like an underwater coffin. He had heard that in one of the tunnels, there were claw marks left by a desperate, dying diver.

Mike's brain flooded with such comforting thoughts as "I'm an idiot! What was I thinking? I could die!" In his frozen state, he wondered if he should choose *fight* or *flight*. At that moment, fleeing sounded excellent to him. But he'd come so far, and he wanted to notch this dive on his experience belt. He wanted to write about it. But his personal chorus of self-doubt was ringing in his ears. Could he do this dangerous thing? Was it too dangerous? *Should* he do it? Was he a lunatic with a death wish, as a lot of people had felt free to inform him? Maybe he should just admit that he was terrified, give up, swim back to shore, and turn in his scuba gear.

In the dark lake, Michael treaded water, putting off the moment of decision, worrying and thinking, "What have I got myself into *this* time? I don't want to go back, but I'm too scared to go forward. What the hell am I going to do now?"

He wasn't the first writer ever to ask himself that question.

We all spend time treading water, though usually not

as literally as Mike. It's the ambiguous, doubtful, delaying, indecisive quality of this step that inspired us to call it "wavering."

Will You or Won't You?

Remember the old song? *First you say you will, and then you won't. Then you say you do, and then you don't. You're undecided now. So what are you gonna do?*

Wavering. As a teenager might say, "It sucks."

To which we'd only add—at least, at this point—"Big time."

Wavering seems to arrive when it's least expected and least welcome. Certainly, you'd never willingly invite it, but surprise, here it is. Such as when you're forty pages into a book and you thought it was going to be smooth sailing from here on out, but now you're stuck. Or like when you've submitted your poems to magazines and you're feeling really good and hopeful about them— until the rejection letters start coming in. Or like when you've arranged to write for a couple of hours every day, and then other responsibilities crop up, just when you thought you had them beaten down.

"It's not fair," we can hear you protest, and who could blame you? You endured that miserable "precreative" state of anxiety, restlessness, and discontent. You let yourself really want to write something. You felt sure you were totally committed to it. And now this, doubt and fear, just when you thought you had those beasts conquered. We can hear you objecting, "You said everything would be OK now. You said I could write if I really wanted to and committed myself to it. But look what's happening to me now. I feel awful again. You said it would be OK now, and it isn't."

No, we didn't, and yes, it is. Everything's still OK, if not quite wonderful. You've done very well to get this far. Really, you have. You're just a little further down the path, that's all. Forgive us for not fully warning you about this step, although you'll have to admit we dropped hints. "Terror, laughter, tears, jeers," remember? If you had actually believed those hints, you might never have started down this path at all.

This step is one of the hardest parts of being a writer, or of being anything worthwhile. Sometimes, it's as hard as a grizzly in your path, and sometimes, it's only a fallen branch that you can step over. But whatever it is, bear or branch, deep or shallow water, it's an obstacle that jerks you out of your perfect dream of writing and back into reality. It's as if you've been strolling blissfully along with a smile on your face, when suddenly, there's a deep growl back in the woods.

But why is this happening now, of all times, just when you were starting to feel so sure of yourself?

It's happening because wavering is a natural part of the writing process. And it's happening now because this is exactly the right time for it. After unhappiness, after wanting, after commitment, after all of that, comes wavering.

The Look of Wavering

Imagine a pot of water you've put on to boil.

When you turn up the heat under the pan, the first thing that happens is that the molecules at the bottom start to expand. As they expand, they lighten and the water rises. As it rises to the top, it cools again, the molecules contract and get heavier, and the water falls back toward the bottom, where it gets heated again. Over and over this happens, until the water at the top begins to get as hot as the water at the bottom. When that happens, it breaks up that nice, even pattern of rising and falling. At that point, a wobble—or waver—develops in the water on top, just prior to actual boiling.

In science, that's the process of "convection."

In writing, that's a picture of what happens after we heat up our wanting, commit ourselves to proceeding, and then develop a wobble on top—in our heads, where the fear and doubts are.

Suddenly, where once you felt so sure, now you've got doubts, just as Michael did in that lake. And speaking of water, maybe you've got these doubts because a little cold water has been splashed on you, or even a bucket of it. Maybe you've seen skeptical looks on other people's faces when you've told them what you want to do with your writing. Maybe you've received some rejections or criticism. Maybe you've been thinking that taking this much time for yourself doesn't fit with your core values of what makes a good person. Or maybe you've felt a weakening of your knees, will, and heart because the writing looks too hard or it will take too long or you can't afford to do it. Or maybe you've really tried to write something, and maybe you were even cookin', but now all of your creative juices have boiled over, and the pan's dried out.

It happens. Believe it or not, there are logical reasons for this misery.

Frank Goodman informs me, this morning, that he has concluded not to go on with the party, saying he has seen danger enough.

—John Wesley Powell

Who Wouldn't Waver?

Bobbie J. A. Pfeifer and her husband took a second mortgage on their house to pay for her trip to a writers conference. She had been selected to attend on the basis of the quality of written work she had submitted; she was one of only 150 writers chosen out of almost a thousand applicants. It felt like an honor to be selected; it felt like vindication of her writing ambitions. But it was also going to be an expensive trip. When she accepted the invitation, it symbolized a huge commitment, a commitment as big as her desire to publish a novel and her husband's desire to help her do it.

And then Bobbie stepped onto step four in the cruelest possible way.

Almost the first thing that happened to her when she arrived at the conference of her dreams was that the organizers handed back to her the sample of her writing that she had submitted for critique, the sample that she thought was good enough to get her there. Scrawled across the top of it, in big, red block letters, was the verdict of the famous writer who had critiqued it: "This will never be published!" Bobbie remembers that it looked "as if he had dug into the paper with his red pen to put the dot on that exclamation mark." Her story looked as if it was "dripping in blood."

She was devastated, as who wouldn't have been in her shoes?

"I've spent all our money to come," she thought, as she stood there shaking and near tears. "I thought they invited me because they liked my writing. My husband has sacrificed for me. My family is so proud, and they're so excited for me to have this opportunity. What will I tell them now?"

This will never be published!

At that time, Bobbie was "just" a wife and mom from the middle of Kansas. She was a long way from home, in many ways, and she was there alone. She was what is sometimes derisively called a "wanna-be writer." She had dreams and desires, she had tons of commitment—enough to get her this far—but she didn't have enough

You cannot do good work if you take your mind off of work to see how the community is taking it.
—Dorothy L. Sayers

writing experience to save her from that collision with a famous writer. She believed what the famous writer—any famous writer—predicted; she didn't know enough to refute his opinion. It wasn't her fault that she walked into a crossroads and a truck hit her, bruised her and threw her back. She thought she'd looked both ways. But that truck was coming faster and harder than she could ever have anticipated, and when it hit her, it did more than knock the wind out of her.

When Bobbie happily, eagerly, nervously reached out her hand to get her critique—and drew back a bloody stub—she was so shocked that she couldn't even move for a few minutes. Her courage and excitement deflated as if the famous writer had stuck a pin in her. She held back her tears. She didn't want to crumble; she wanted to be strong. Somehow, she found the fortitude to squeak, "Why?"

His blunt, cold answer flabbergasted her.

"You're unpublished, right? First-person stories are considered so difficult to carry for a full novel that inexperienced, nonpublished writers such as yourself aren't likely to pull it off. It'll be rejected at the get-go."

Bobbie had never heard of such a thing, and for good reason—many, many first novels that get published are written in the first person.

Somehow, she made it through the rest of the conference, even nabbing an agent for herself with that same story the famous writer had condemned to unpublished perdition. (One man's poison is another man's publishable manuscript.) And somehow, when she got back home, she rewrote her book based on other comments he made. But she hated what she did on his advice. Eventually, Bobbie shredded all of those revisions and threw the pieces away. She stopped writing for six months, too depressed and full of self-doubt to go on.

Bobbie was having herself a horrible case of wavering, all based on illusion.

Maybe Bobbie was lucky that it lasted "only" six months. That kind of early discouragement from a respected authority figure has kept many writers stuck for years in a kind of step four purgatory.

It happened to Nancy when she was a senior in college.

"I took the only creative writing course of my life," she recalls. "Our first assignment was to write a short story. On the day the teacher came back with our grades, he read my story aloud to the class—to make fun of it. He led the class in laughing at it. He didn't divulge the name of the author, so I sat there pretending to laugh along with the rest of them at my own work, while I was dying inside. Because I was immature, both as a person and as a writer, it didn't occur to me that his response said more about him than it did about my writing. Instead, I took it to mean that I had no talent for fiction. I'd always 'known' I didn't have any imagination; his opinion just confirmed that for me. It would be fifteen years before I would seriously try my hand at writing stories again."

Seventeen published novels and scores of published short stories later, Nancy is here to tell you she survived. We hope you will, too, if such a thing ever happens to you. It isn't easy to get over something like that when you're young, naive, inexperienced, or just unsure of yourself, but many writers have had to do it. (And who *is* sure of himself when he's just starting out, at any age? It's the rare writer, or person, who can laugh off a critic's scorn or see it for the callous act it is.) Chillingly similar things have happened to many other writers who later went on to become successfully published, among them the best-selling novelist Elizabeth Forsyth Hailey and S. J. Hinton, the prizewinning author of children's books. Both women report having been so cruelly criticized by writing teachers that they stopped writing for years, convinced they had no business ever wanting to be writers.

Those are dramatic instances of what can happen in step four.

It's not always that bad, but it is always about doubt and fear flooding in to drown confidence. According to an ancient source of wisdom, the *I Ching*, the problem is that a bit of decay has set into the situation. That being the case, it's best to be alert for the earliest signs, in order to start cleaning it up before it has a chance to infect your whole creative system.

Perfectionism is self-abuse of the highest order.
—Anne Wilson Schaef

Who's That Wavering at Me in the Mirror?

You'll probably recognize the signs of wavering when you see them in other people, but you may find it harder to spot when it happens to you. It's good to learn to recognize and name it, though. Naming things seems to remove some of the fear of them, and naming them— "Oh, yeah, I'm wavering"—reminds you that these are only steps, and everybody goes through them.

This step can look like shock, paralysis, immobility, as if you've just been electrocuted or slapped with a dead fish. It can look like procrastination or writer's block. It can look like pacing up and down, like sitting down and getting up and sitting down and getting up again. It can look like doubt in your eyes, furrows in your brow, biting your lower lip in worry. It can look like chewed fingernails, raw cuticles, chain-smoked cigarettes, an empty cartoon of cookie-dough ice cream that you ate all by yourself, or too many drinks. It can look like snapping at your children, hiding your head under the covers, going on a shopping binge, or sitting for hours staring despondently out a window. It can look like a person who can't make up his mind or follow through.

It looks like Bobbie, rooted to the spot with the critique in her hand.

It looks like Nancy, pinned to her chair by the mocking words of her teacher.

It looks like Thomas Dewey, who went to bed one night thinking he was the new president of the United States and woke up the next morning to headlines suggesting that maybe he wasn't, after all.

It looks and feels like, Oh, shit. Oh, dear. Oh, no. What if? What now?

It looks like a *Peanuts* cartoon: In the first frame, Snoopy is asleep on his back on top of his doghouse. Next, he's jolted awake. Next, he's sitting up, thinking, "There I was, sleeping comfortably." And finally, he's lying back down and thinking, "Suddenly I was plagued by a self-doubt."

What do you look like when you're struck by doubt?

If you're not sure, ask somebody who knows you well enough to describe how you behave when you're scared. How might you act, for instance, if you were Michael treading water in that lake? Do you think you would freeze with fear, or would you thrash around like a harpooned whale?

Nancy has a friend who told her, "When you're scared, you get very quiet."

We have a writer friend who speaks of herself as going into a "spin" in which she compulsively moves furniture and paints walls and just can't stop. She looks very

We would worry less about what others think of us if we realized how seldom they do.

—Ethel Barrett

busy, but she'd be the first to admit that she's doing nothing to fulfill her writing commitment.

Those are clues to the appearance and feeling of this step. When you find yourself unable to move or unable to stop moving, consider the possibility that you're wavering about something.

You'll probably find that wavering is a combination of compulsive movement *and* paralysis. On the one hand, you can't seem to stop doing what you don't want to do, but on the other hand, you can't seem to get yourself to do what you feel you should do. These two manifestations of wavering look different from each other, but they have an identical result—no forward movement. You can be frozen or you can be spinning, but either way, you're stuck.

Another clue to the fact that you're wavering is the appearance of the dreaded "yes, buts." *Yes, I'd like to write, but I don't have time. Yes, I'd like to get published, but I'm afraid to send out my stuff. Yes, I'd go to that writers conference, but I can't afford it. Yes, I wish I could write on weekends, but my family needs me. Yes, I'd write, but everybody knows that good writers never get published. Yes, I'd like to write, but I don't know how. Yes, I love romances, but I'd be embarrassed to write one. Yes, I wrote a first draft, but I hate to rewrite. Yes, I sent out some poems, but they got rejected, so I'm never doing that again.* For more experienced writers, the "yes, buts" might sound more like *Yes, I've been writing nonstop for six weeks and I'm exhausted, but I can't afford to take a break. Yes, I want to try something different, but my publisher won't let me. Yes, I'm sick of journalism and I want to write a novel, but I've got to earn a living.*

Paralyzed. Spinning. Yes, but. They are symptoms of wavering.

Fortunately, there's a cure.

*He who forecasts
all perils will
never sail the sea.*
—Anonymous

When Doubt Is a Good Thing

Yes, I have doubted. I have wandered off the path, but I always return. It is intuitive, an intrinsic, built-in sense of direction. I seem always to find my way home.

—Helen Hayes

The doubts we have about ourselves as writers, about our prospects, or about any given writing project are not always bad things. Doubts and fears can serve a valuable purpose; they're not intrinsically negative. Seeing the good in your wavering could be the first step toward your cure. A doubt is like a nerve that signals pain, only in the case of doubt, it signals cause for concern about what you're doing. The nerve in your finger announces, "This stove is hot!" It knows what it's talking about. The doubt in your head may be trying to tell you, "This idea won't work, after all," and it may know what it's talking about, too. It's hard to face facts like that, but the truth is, maybe your idea really *isn't* big enough for a whole book; maybe it should be a short story, instead. Maybe your work really isn't ready for prime time; maybe you could benefit from more practice. Maybe this draft isn't as good as it should be; maybe it could stand to be rewritten one more time. Those may be hard facts to face at the time, but they are surely good things to know in the long run. Writers who deny them—by denying reality or by bulling their way through it—will run up against bigger problems later when they'll be even harder to handle.

"I backed out of writing a novel the first time I tried it," Nancy recalls. "This was a couple of years before I made my commitment to write fiction full-time. In that earlier attempt, I had a wonderful time writing the first few chapters. I was downright gleeful. But then I began to waver. I saw that there was a lot of hard work ahead, not just fun, and I wasn't sure I could manage it or even if I wanted to. I had second thoughts about devoting that much of my life to a book, and so I decided to stop writing it. I felt a little regret but, honestly, not much. It was the right decision. I wasn't ready."

She says there have been other times when she wasn't so smart.

"I remember one time in particular when I got a chance to live in Fort Lauderdale for six weeks one winter. I took my computer with me and forced myself to write five pages a day on my new novel, even though nothing I was doing with the book felt right. I had serious doubts about it. It wasn't so much that I was writing badly as it was that, intuitively, the whole book just felt *wrong*. Wrong plot, wrong characters, wrong everything. I thought about letting it go and just stopping to enjoy my trip, but no, my Puritan work ethic raised its head and squawked, 'Work!' So I ignored my intuition. When I got home, I read through all those pages that I'd hacked out, and I realized they stank. It was all wasted work, and it really was wasted, because I couldn't even use them to build on. I ended up throwing it all away and starting over. And I thought, 'Damn. I could have been at the beach.' "

On the other hand, your doubts may not be justified at all. Maybe you *do* have a good idea for a novel; maybe your work *is* ready for prime time; maybe you *don't* need another rewrite. "There have been plenty of times," Lynn says, "when I've sent off a query letter, a proposal, a few sample chapters, or even a whole manuscript that I felt really good about when I stuck it in the mail. But then if my agent or editor doesn't get back to me right away, the decay sets in. Doubts eat away at me. I start fretting to my husband that maybe it really isn't any good, maybe I sent it off too soon, and maybe they'll hate

You can't build a reputation on what you are going to do.

—Henry Ford

it. About the time I've practically spun myself into the ground from worrying, I get an E-mail that says they love it. Then I know it was always OK, all the time."

Judith Greber (Gillian Roberts) has also been there, as have most of us. "I'm on an emotional roller coaster during the first draft of a book," she says. "I'm high on it, then in despair. I think it's a fabulous idea; then I know it's drivel. Sometimes, later drafts put me on a better emotional keel, but inevitably, by the time I send the book in, I've seen those words too many times, and I'm back in the slough of despond. I always offer to rip it up and start over again when I mail it to the agent or editor."

It's the not knowing that's so hard. It's our fear of the unknown that gets us. Whatever the answer to our doubts—whether it's yes, no, or maybe—we need to know, if we can possibly find out. If you can't do that—if, like Lynn waiting to hear from her agent, it's a situation over which you have no control—then the secret is to have faith and to manage to hold on while you wait for the answer, like Michael in the lake, treading water until the realization came to him that he really was adequately prepared to make the dive. No, he didn't know precisely what might happen to him in the caverns, any more than any of us knows for sure how an agent or an editor will react to our work or how our characters will react in any given scene or if a poem will end the way we envision it. But when we know as much as we *can* know, when we realize that we've done the best we can, and when we apply that knowledge as a balm to our fears, then our heart finally tells our head that it's time to *move* . . . and we do.

Wavering is a test of our character and our work. And that's just fine, because it strengthens both of them. Surely, it's better to find out now that your wonderful idea for a story really won't stretch as far as a novel than it is to write a whole book and *then* find out. It's better to acknowledge that your poems need more work *before* you send them out and not afterward. It's better to keep some other income flowing in if writing full-time won't pay your rent. It's good to know. Knowing brings relief, and that's oddly true even when the news is bad and doubly true when the news is good.

Sometimes, what you discover is that you're starting to walk down somebody else's path instead of your own . . .

Wavering Your Way to Clarity about Yourself

When Nancy was newly married, her husband bought a partial interest in an airplane.

"I think you should take some flying lessons," he announced to her one horrifying day, "so you can get the plane down if anything ever happens to me."

This was not a welcome suggestion for a woman who was scared of heights, speed, and flying. Thinking she'd finesse her way out of it, she said, "OK, but only if you can find me a female flight instructor." This was 1976, in Kansas. Nancy thought she was safe.

The next day, he handed her the name of a woman who taught flying.

Surprisingly, she loved the lessons. It turned out that she had a bit of a natural feel for flying an airplane. Who'd have thought it? She liked her instructor. She loved studying clouds and weather. She ended up taking twenty hours of flight lessons, and she even soloed in the airplane several times, flying touch-and-goes at the airport, all by herself. She thought she was committed to going the whole way and getting her own pilot's license.

From going from the sublimation of pain to the direct contact with your fear brings the sensation of feeling time, like chewing time, feeling the very essence of being alone for minutes, hours, days and nights.

—Jose Antonio Martinez

He said, "My God, it's amazing and marvelous how you walk with all those hundreds and hundreds of legs. How do you do it? How do you get them all moving that way?" The centipede stopped and thought and said, "Well, I take the left front leg and then I"— and he thought about it for awhile and he couldn't walk.

—Edward Albee

But then two unnerving things happened that set her to wavering.

One afternoon, she was happily doing touch-and-goes with another instructor when he suddenly said to her, "Didn't you hear that?"

"What?" She had no idea what he meant.

"The controller just called you on the radio three times to give you clearance to land. He's waiting for you to confirm. Didn't you hear him?"

She hadn't heard anything. She had been too busy daydreaming, which is a fine habit for a novelist but not so good for a pilot. This incident gave her pause. She couldn't help but remember what had been said about Antoine de Saint-Exupéry, the author of *The Little Prince*. In addition to being a writer, he was a pilot who had walked away from crashes several times. His friend Sarah Murphy observed of him, "He's too much of a poet to be a pilot." It was sadly prophetic, because shortly afterward, Saint-Exupéry died in his final crash.

Maybe flying an airplane isn't such a good idea for daydreamers.

The second thing that decided Nancy against flying was when her instructor told her to go up and do "stalls" by herself. You know what stalls are? They're where you point the nose of the plane up until the warning signal screams and the plane stalls, and then, against all common sense, you keep the nose pointed up until such time as you feel the plane naturally begin to right itself. Needless to say, this maneuver requires sufficient altitude.

That was the day Nancy's wavering stopped, and so did her flying lessons. "This is not for me," she knew at that moment. "I've had a great time, but I'm not taking this any further. This is my husband's hobby, not mine."

She has never regretted that decision. It probably helped her later, when she wavered and then said no to an editor who wanted her to write a series of mysteries that weren't her style. When an agent suggested she write romances, she was able to say no to the extra money that might have earned because she sensed it would "stall her out" on her way to becoming a mystery writer.

If you ever find yourself flying somebody else's airplane—or living somebody else's life—then wavering gives you the chance to land safely and get back on solid ground again. It's a much better option than crashing.

Sometimes, wavering saves our lives, our careers, our relationships.

It's perfectly honorable to back down. If you get the feeling that something's not right for you, or the timing's not right for you, trust your own gut. You don't even have to try again if you don't want to. You'll know that's the right decision if you feel relief upon making it and you don't regret it very much later.

Usually, however, wavering isn't about telling you it's time to stop. A lot of times, wavering happens because in the passion of step two (Wanting) and the excitement of step three (Commitment), we somehow manage to overlook a few things. Like the fact that it takes months or years to write a book, and we can't just do it overnight. Or that it takes a long time to establish yourself as a writer, and you can't usually expect to support yourself immediately. Or that even the best ideas need time to be developed and to gestate. Or that merely deciding to be a writer doesn't actually make you one. Little things like that. Certain small matters that we may have overlooked up to now.

Now they crash in on us, demanding to be considered.

Novelists run into this about forty pages into a book when they realize that one idea does not a whole book make. "Oh, my God, this is hard work," they suddenly remember, as Nancy also found out the hard way. "I'm actually going to have to think about this plot. Maybe I should do some outlining. I'm going to have to think about these characters, too. And my first chapter sucks." It looked like fun when they started out in that first flush of enthusiasm, but now they're wavering.

Poets may get all the way through a stanza and then start to worry that it's trite.

Journalists may research an article that doesn't seem to come together.

Amateurs do it and pros do it. We all do it. We waver.

Those kinds of wavering may not get a writer stuck for long, however. If you have the experience to know it's normal, or a finely honed sense of intuition, or if you have the eagerness of a beginner, you may sail right over those rough spots.

But sometimes, it gets a lot harder.

You Are Stuck Here. But Why?

In her counseling practice, Lynn has observed that wavering gets problematic for four main reasons—unfair comparison, perfectionism, catastrophizing, and a lack of accurate information. To which Nancy adds her own personal favorite, which she calls "getting too big for my britches," and its evil twin, "biting off less than I can chew." They're all a kind of denial of the truth. Lynn calls them dark holes along the writing path, like caves you shouldn't enter. Stick your head carelessly into any of them, she warns, and you'll find yourself facing the writerly equivalent of a poisonous snake or a hornets' nest.

Want a bad case of wavering?

Just stick your head down the comparison hole—by unfairly comparing yourself or your writing to other writers or to your own last work—and prepare to get stung. "Unfairly" means comparing apples with oranges, or apple seeds with full-grown apples. It's comparing the fact-based article you wrote for your local newspaper to the lyricism of your friend's poetry. Apples and oranges. Or it's comparing your first mystery to Sue Grafton's tenth one. Apple seeds and full-grown apples.

It's fine, inspirational, and motivational to read the best writing in order to give ourselves something high at which to aim. But it's not fine—it's dispiriting and unmotivating—to compare our work unfairly. Any of us would feel wounded if somebody else did that to us, so why do it to ourselves?

When we have no picture of how something should be, then we can be innocently happy with how it is, whatever it is. A little kid just loves to bounce a ball; she doesn't know from scores and fouls. A beginning writer just loves to pour out words; he doesn't know the "rules." But the minute they start comparing themselves with how the big kids do it, suddenly they may feel intimidated and less capable. They may not feel so sure that they want to play, at least not where the big kids can see how the ball—or the writing—gets away from them sometimes.

When we compare our performance to some perceived standard—and standards are always subjective—we set ourselves up for wavering. At writers conferences, for instance, we see painful moments when a "baby writer" grows self-conscious as he compares himself to writers who have more experience than he. By sticking his nose in the hole of comparison, he gets bitten by

Have no fear of perfection—you'll never reach it.
—Salvador Dalí

self-doubt. By the end of the conference, some of those beginners who came with such innocent joy and exuberance in their writing are feeling like failures, when they have only just begun to learn how to write.

If you nurse a belief that you aren't good enough, you'll generate self-doubt. Comparison is a perpetual self-doubt machine, guaranteed to hold you prisoner for as long as you run it. Self-doubt feeds on comparisons. Keep it up long enough and you should develop a lovely case of writer's block or at least a case of galloping procrastination.

"If I'm working on a book," Nancy says, about comparison, "and I start reading another work of fiction and it is so good that it inspires me, I'll keep reading. I love the way Dick Francis opens his mysteries, for instance, and reading them always inspires me to try harder. But if what I'm reading is so good that it depresses me, making me feel that everything I write is crap, then I stop reading that book immediately. It's bad for me and bad for my writing. Inspiration's one thing, but comparison is something else entirely, and you know what? Sometimes, it may hit me hard, not because the writing's so much better than anything I could do but just because of something as stupid as forgetting to eat lunch and getting a bout of low blood sugar that depresses my mood and increases my vulnerability. It's not worth it. If I'm comparing myself and starting to feel bad about it, I put distance between me and whatever or whomever I'm comparing myself to."

Lynn adds, "Sometimes, when I'm comparing myself to another writer and feeling bad about it, the only thing that's the matter with me is that I'm tired, and all I need is a nap. Or sometimes, a shower can snap me out of it. I

I realize that if I wait until I am no longer afraid to act, write, speak, be, I'll be sending messages on a Ouija board, cryptic complaints from the other side.

—Audre Lorde

try to recognize those times when I'm physically vulnerable, so that I won't open the comparison door and fall through a hole in my ego."

We've all fallen prey to comparing ourselves unfairly. Sometimes, we even make ourselves feel bad by comparing our latest work—usually, a rough draft—to our previous finished work. That's so unfair.

Best-selling novelist John Lescroart manages to put a positive spin on that dangerous habit, by using comparison to spur himself on to new heights, but it's not easy even for him. "I ask myself when beginning a new book, how will I write another story better than this last one?" he says. "It's a little upsetting, but I have to overcome it. I don't even know what story I'm going to tell, but I'd better start writing it. Why don't I just start? That's what I've got to do. So I start five scenes and throw them all away. My biggest surprise is finding out how hard it is to beat my last effort. When you are expected to produce a quality book every year, it gets pretty intense."

If comparison is that tricky even for him, imagine the danger for most of us.

Stick your head in the *comparison* hole, and you'll get bitten.

Fall into the *perfectionism* hole, and you'll plunge into space.

If you're like most of us, you could probably dump on yourself a hundred times a day about how your writing isn't good enough. But what *is* "good enough," anyway? Who draws that line in the dirt, and why does it seem to keep moving on us?

How about adopting a new standard, something along the lines of "as good as I can get it right now." That's actually a very high standard, when you think about it, because it takes hard work to get a piece of writing to a place at which you can honestly say it's as good as you can get it at this time.

"That's what I aim for with a novel," Nancy admits. "I know it's ready to send to my editor when it feels that it's as good as I can get it at this time, all things considered." Those "things" that she considers include her ability, her experience, and the amount of time she has to write the book. Like anybody else, Nancy would love to have a perfect manuscript to mail off, but the truth is, she's never had one yet, and she's never going to have one, and neither are you, because perfection is the impossible dream.

If "perfection" is a goal that motivates you, that's fine. Sue Grafton, for instance, says she hopes one day to write a perfect mystery, and that inspires her to keep working on her craft. If it doesn't paralyze you, then you don't have a problem with it. For most writers, however, a quest for perfection is counterproductive, because it pokes a stick in the wheel of their progress, slowing them down or throwing them over their own handlebars. For those writers, it takes more courage to be willing to live with imperfection than to aim for perfection. Twelve-step programs like Alcoholics Anonymous advise focusing on progress, not perfection. That's good advice for most writers, too.

Nora Roberts has a great suggestion for any writer suffering from a bad case of perfectionism: be willing to write badly. "I can fix a bad page," she points out, "but I can't fix a blank one." To which romance writer Susan Elizabeth Phillips adds, "I found the courage to fill my screen with bad pages on those days when my mind was mush, then trusted myself to fix them later."

Progress, not perfection: that's one way to get over wavering.

Catastrophizing is another dark cave on the path. It's accompanied by doom and gloom and words like *never* and *always*. "I'll never be able to do it." "It's always going to be this way." "I can't ever." "They won't ever." "Nobody will." "Everybody does." It speaks in generalities, and that means it's usually wrong. Hardly anything in this world is never, always, or totally this or completely that. If you think it is, you're on a sure route to wavering about whatever it is you want to do with your writing.

We catastrophize because we're afraid of the unknown, like a certain little rabbit who came up out of his hole one day, looked around, and exclaimed, "Oh, what a lovely day! I think I'll go for a romp. But what if the fox eats me? I wish I could decide—"

CHOMP.

That's why we're afraid of the unknown, because it may jump out and eat us. That's certainly why some writers never start and others never finish and some only go half as far as they could go. We're scared, and who can blame us? No less a writer than Stephen King has said that writing is like crossing the Atlantic Ocean in a bathtub, so is it any wonder that it occasionally scares the pants off the rest of us?

You can see from that little fable, however, that wavering can also get you eaten.

So when you're afraid of the unknown, should you go ahead and leap in or hang back and think about it? A wise old rabbit says, when afraid of the unknown, avoid extremes of behavior. Neither overimpulsive nor overdeliberate be.

The fourth dark cave that Lynn has observed in her counseling practice is a simple—or sometimes not so simple—*lack of information*.

The real secret of patience is to find something to do in the meantime.

—*Dell Pencil Puzzles and Word Games*

Remember our story about Bobbie, who was flooded with doubt when the famous writer said her story would never be published because she had written it in the first person? All Bobbie lacked was one small piece of information—that he was wrong, wrong, wrong. She might have figured that out—and recovered from wavering sooner—if she'd asked a few other professionals or checked out some novels to see if any were written in the first person or researched books about publishing. Remember the story about how Nancy was demoralized by the teacher who made fun of her writing? She might have saved herself fifteen years of wavering if she'd had the courage to spill out her feelings to her friends, who might have pointed out to her that she was only a beginner, after all, and he was a jerk.

Additional information can be a wonderful thing.

Novelists frequently get blocked, only to realize later that they just need to do more research for their book. Then, once they have in hand the facts they need to finish the story, they're off and running again. The same thing happens to other kinds of writers, too. So when in doubt, or when blocked in your writing, at least consider the possibility that it may be telling you that you just need to get more information. Be brave and ask questions. Look things up. Get thee to a library. It might work a miracle cure on your wavering.

Getting too big for my britches—Nancy's favorite way of plunging herself into wavering—is a dark hole that may be related to both unfair comparison and perfectionism, but we think it deserves its own category.

It happens when you start thinking too big.

"I can think of several examples from my own life," Nancy admits. "When I signed a contract with Scribners, I was paralyzed by the fact that they were the leg-

It's beginnings that are hard. I always begin with a great sense of dread and trepidation. Nietzsche says that the decision to start writing is like leaping into a cold lake.

—Susan Sontag

endary publishers of Fitzgerald, Hemingway, Faulkner, and Wolfe. For days, I couldn't even write for thinking about that, until one day I said out loud, 'I'm just writing a mystery, for heaven's sake. You guys go haunt Joyce Carol Oates.' I don't know if they did—she doesn't seem to ever be blocked—but they left me alone after that. I was thinking too big for my britches. I didn't have to worry one little bit about being as good as F. Scott Fitzgerald."

She recalls another way she falls into that trap. "When I'm facing a tough deadline, I can get overwhelmed by how much I have to write—or rewrite—and how little time there is to do it. Then I'll go lie down on my bed and stare hopelessly at the ceiling and think about how to tell my son that we have to sell our house, until I remember Anne Lamott's advice, in her book *Bird by Bird*, to break it down into manageable pieces.

" 'Word by word, Nancy,' I remind myself then. 'You don't have to write the whole thing all at once. Just take it sentence by sentence, scene by scene.' Once I remember that, I get up and focus on a single small scene, and I start to write again."

Sometimes, we waver, though, not because the challenge seems too big but because it seems too small. That's why we call this one *biting off less than I can chew*. It happens when you get into something, only to discover that it feels bland, boring, tasteless, meaningless, or even against your principles. If the cure for Nancy was to think smaller, the cure for this bout of wavering is to think bigger, because what you're trying to write is apparently smaller than you are. So either think of a way to bring it up to your size or put it aside for a bigger challenge that better suits your abilities or your conscience.

Lynn once experienced a situation in which she got to

see three writers all wavering at once, and all for different reasons. "It was ugly," she says with a shudder. "We
were, supposedly, gathered together to finish a project,
but then three sticks got stuck into three spokes. One of
us said, 'I didn't know we were supposed to do it all this
weekend, and besides, I don't even like our format.'
That was lack of information at work and probably perfectionism, too. The second writer said, 'Format, schmor-
mat, I'm not touching anything that smells of self-help.'
That was biting off less than he could chew. He needed
to find a way to make it feel important enough to him.
The third one—me—wailed, 'But you promised!' Beneath that wail was my old friend catastrophizing, something I'm pretty good at doing, having practiced it many
times over the years."

They worked it out by providing enough information
("Yes, we can get most of it done this weekend, and here's
how"), by working until it was "good enough," by making sure that the material held enough significance, and
by Lynn's speaking the truth to the others about how
much other work she was facing and about how those
three days were all she had to give them. Then, with the
increased faith in one another that comes from truth, they
let go of their wavering behaviors and set to work again.

"And *that* was beautiful," Lynn says.

Wavering is an uncomfortable place to be, but there's
a cure for it—and that is truth and faith, which some
people may consider to be an odd combination, indeed.

A Test of Your Mettle

As we said earlier, wavering is a necessary test of your
character and your work. Is it ready for the next step?
Are you? It's as if there's a troll under a bridge on your

path, and he jumps out and bellows, "Who goes there?" He's horribly ugly and fierce-looking, and he's not going to let you pass unless you can prove you're worthy to go on.

"I discovered the existence of these trolls," Nancy says, "when I read *The Writer's Journey*, by Christopher Vogler. He called them 'Guardians of the Threshold,' and he suggested that they are any obstacle that stands between us and what we want. They could be illness, poverty, opposition, self-doubt, perfectionism, inexperience, ignorance, unfair comparison—virtually anything that appears to stop us."

Trolls, in other words. They often appear on this and other steps along the writer's path.

Soon after reading that book, Nancy was scheduled to take a solo car trip across the Great Plains. She had never taken such a long car journey by herself before, and she was nervous about it. "The day I was supposed to go, I woke up with a bad stomachache. I was just about to cancel the trip when it occurred to me that this could be one of those damned trolls. Maybe it was only my fear that was causing my stomachache. I realized the only way I'd know for sure was if I went ahead and started my trip. Either I'd get sicker, or I wouldn't. Well, about three hours down the road, as I was gobbling up cherry pie in a little café in a small town in Kansas, I realized I felt great. No more stomachache. It had been a troll, testing my mettle for this adventure that was going to stretch me a bit. I felt really good then, to know that I'd proved my worthiness to go on."

There are all manner of trolls in the writing biz: Agents who turn you down, editors who reject you, critique groups who demoralize you, illnesses that sidetrack you, bills that overwhelm you, ideas that go flat,

When I am most doubtful about my writing is when I read a first draft and I realize it's not a keeper. That is a perfectly awful moment!

—Nina Osier

sentences that won't sing, and doubt that assails you. They may scare you to death or infuriate you or leave you feeling beaten, but don't let them fool you entirely. All they really want is for you to present your writerly credentials of courage, a willingness to learn and to face the truth, true humility, hard work, and realistic self-confidence. Show them all of that, and eventually, even if it takes a while, they'll have to wave you through.

Like the frog who turns into a prince when you kiss him, that troll will become invisible as you pass through him. And if you don't? If he continues to look as real and dangerous as a troll? If he still won't accept your credentials and turns you away? Then fall back, regroup, check to make sure you really do have your credentials in order, and try again. Maybe next time, he'll let you pass.

There will always be trolls; there will always be other chances to prove yourself—and every encounter with a troll will strengthen you, if it doesn't kill you first.

When It Isn't Wavering

Be advised that there's a "problem" that writers run into that can be confused with wavering, but it's not. It's not actually a problem at all, unless we turn it into one. It's *waiting*, which we also talked about in an earlier chapter. This kind of waiting has to do with timing, but not the actual clock time you need for writing. This is more existential than that, having to do with whether or not the *writing* wants to be written right now. You're not always the one in charge, you know. The piece on which you're working has something to say about things, too. And if that sounds bizarre, all we can tell you is that longtime writers know exactly what we mean. Sometimes, ideas and writing just need a little time to percolate or to sim-

My sister came in, looked at me sitting at my typewriter on a fine Maine day and said, "Are you sure you're not depressed? Why aren't you out doing things with people instead of sitting here alone doing nothing?" She really did make me wonder if there was something wrong with me. I put the work away and didn't go near it for a decade.

—Nina Osier

mer. Sometimes, you write so hard and so well that you drain the well of your creativity and it just needs a little time to fill back up again.

When that happens, you're not wavering, you're waiting.

Remember how, back in step one, we heard Lia Matera describe how she paints during the periods when she's waiting for her real writing to emerge? By doing something creative, she keeps her motor running.

That's a good thing to do in periods of either wavering or waiting.

Nancy describes a time in between projects when she wasn't wavering, and the waiting was a kind of cooling-off period. She went on a wild creative binge that had nothing to do with her next book but that used up all the excess energy she needed to burn. As she said in an E-mail to Lynn, "After mailing off my novel, I thought I'd plunge right into our book, but I found I was drained, exhausted, and so full of end-of-book electricity and anxiety that I couldn't sleep. I was waking up at 2:30, 4:30, getting maybe three hours of sleep a night, in no shape to work on something important. So in four days' time, I wrote two six-thousand-word short stories that were due, respectively, on November 1 and December 1. Got those out of the way and approved. Then I totally cleaned out my basement, then my garage, then my guest room, then my winter coat closet, then the closet with a decade's worth of Christmas wrapping. All the time feeling anxiety and guilt because I wasn't working on our book but also knowing I was probably doing the best thing, all things considered, including how fast I can write when I have to."

Notice that even while waiting, Nancy is quite productive.

"Sometimes," she corrects. "Other times, I wait like sloths wait."

"Delay is natural to a writer," E. B. White said. "He is like a surfer—he bides his time, waits for the perfect wave on which to ride in. Delay is instinctive with him. He waits for the surge that will carry him along."

That's all well and good in theory, especially if you have a rich spouse or a trust fund to see you through—and don't we all?—but meanwhile, your book is due, or some decision awaits you. What "should" you do while you're delaying, while you're weighing options, while you're working up your courage or seeking other opinions? We suggest you take a hint from Lia Matera and find an outlet for your pent-up creativity that will keep it rolling until such time as you're through wavering or waiting.

Sometimes, it doesn't take that much effort, though.

A lot of writers confess that when they're stuck, they get their best ideas while taking a shower or playing solitaire or taking a walk.

If none of those things springs you loose, you may want to try some things that Lynn "prescribes" to the most seriously stuck of her clients.

"Sometimes, clients come in who have been stuck too long," she says. "They look like bedraggled, starving, thirsty travelers. Their depression has already reached such a deep point that it takes something dramatic, almost absurd, to bring them out of it. Or they have waited for so long in such apathy and lethargy that it's all they can do to sit upright in my office, much less come up with a plan of action for themselves. With these folks, I sometimes have to take extreme measures to pump some life back in."

What she does is let them know that they're killing

themselves. In our criminal justice system, that's called attempted murder. And what do we do with people who attempt to kill other people? Forget about extracting promises of better behavior. They're way past that and nearly incapable of keeping any promises. Forget about making deals with them or drawing up "contracts." If we catch them in time, before the deed is done, the only thing left to do is to sentence them. And that's what Lynn tells her clients to do: as long as they're already in "jail," she says, they may as well sentence themselves to the metaphorical equivalent of making license plates or pounding rocks. The idea is that if you're *sentenced*, you have to do it. For some strange reason, putting it that way actually seems to work with some people, although usually only the most desperate ones.

In this "courtroom," we have a system of "alternative sentencing."

There's a lot of creative leeway here, so if you're in these dire straits, take your pick of any of the following:

A writer takes earnest measure to secure his solitude and then finds endless ways to squander it.
—Don DeLillo

• Set a timer and write for five, ten, fifteen, or twenty minutes without stopping, once a day. Doodle for the whole time if that's all you can manage, or write gibberish, but keep your pen or computer going the whole time without any interruption. No E-mails, no conversations, no stopping until the timer goes off.

• Make a date with a responsible friend who will not let you down and write together in the same space. Her house, your house, a park, a restaurant, whatever. Nancy used to go over to a friend's apartment on Saturdays, and they'd each write in separate rooms for an hour, then take a ten-minute break for tea and talk, and then go write for another hour. Then they'd read their work to each other. Give each other topics if you want to. Pull topics out of a hat. Open a magazine, point blindly to a sentence, and write about that. Or draw those circles or write that gibberish if that's all you can manage. Eventually, it will turn into words. It really will.

• Print out all of your E-mails between you and your best friend and read them. You may have a story, a poem, or an article there, and you didn't even know it.

• Get a book with writing exercises in it, and do them. Nancy once did every single one of the exercises in Gabriele Rico's wonderful workbook *Writing the Natural Way*. Another time, she did all of the exercises in one of Lawrence Block's terrific books about writing. It's fun to do this, and you'll feel good about yourself when you're done.

• Write the following words on your computer screen or a notebook and see what follows them: "If I could write about something right now, what I'd really like to write about is . . ." Next time, write this, and see what happens: "If I were going to tell the truth about something that I've never told before, it would be . . ." The third time, write: "What I really hate, loathe, and can't stand is . . ." The fourth time, write: "If people only knew how much I love . . ." And the fifth time, write: "I wish I could talk to somebody who would understand and tell them about . . ."

Those are all honorable, constructive things to do while you're waiting or wavering, if you can't quite manage painting a picture, taking piano lessons, coaching a soccer team, or planting a garden while your mind decides or your creativity percolates. They will help to keep your motor running and maybe even get you out of "park."

Creativity doesn't move in a straight line, nor does it follow the clock. If it were that straightforward, it would be mere spelling and typing, not writing. Creativity rarely moves with complete ease from first idea to final execution. It starts, it stops, it stutters. Sometimes, it glides, and that's bliss, but other times, it screeches to a halt, and that can be hell. Only rarely does a writer get so good at riding the wave that she can feel the underlying pattern of its ebb and flow.

Experienced artists of every kind liken creativity to a well that fills and then empties. Creativity percolates, like water and coffee. Try to write from a dry well and all you'll get is dust. Try to drink coffee before it's fully perked and you'll spit out a weak and tasteless brew. As creators, as writers, we have to learn to feel, to sense, to intuit, to wait—or accept the consequences of lesser work.

And here's an even more vivid metaphor to consider. If you were to open a cocoon, do you know what you'd find inside? Liquid. Caterpillars dissolve during their metamorphosis into butterflies. Sometimes, the same is true of our writing. It starts out feeling solid, but then it seems to retreat into a cocoon. We have to wait then and resist the urge to try to open it up again prematurely. Our reward for such patience will be writing that has metamorphosed into something stronger, more beautiful, and mature.

Waiting is not the same as wavering, but you can cope with them in similar ways.

As for wavering—it isn't fun, but it isn't fatal and it isn't forever.

How to Take the Wobble out of Your Waver

This step is all about separating illusion from reality, and that can be tricky. If you were walking in the desert and saw a mirage, you wouldn't know if it was real or imagined until you got there. But of course, in this fourth step, you don't really *want* to get there, because it might actually be a mirage, and it might be guarded by dangerous and evil creatures who will eat you in one bite. But take it from us, you need to keep moving anyway, even if you sing at the top of your lungs, wear a bell around your neck, or clang pots and pans together while you do.

If you are ready to face those trolls, there's a simple way to tell if your doubts and fears are realistic.

Let's say, for instance, that you've got an idea for a poem—or an article or a story—but you're not sure about it. You could just plunge in and see what happens, or you could ask yourself, "Where do I want my writer's path to lead me?" This question serves as a reminder of your most basic values, desires, and goals. Next, ask yourself, "Will this idea lead me to that result?" If it will, you have your answer. If it won't, you also have your answer. You can rephrase that question to cover any situation over which you're wavering: "Will this decision lead me to that result?" "Will this agent, this editor, this procrastination, this perfectionism, this place, this person, this book lead me where I want my writer's path to take me?"

At the moment of writing this book, Nancy has written proposals for two different novels, and she is feeling unsure of which one she "should" do. Both ideas excite her. But when Lynn asks her, "Where do you want your writer's path to lead you?" and Nancy answers, "To where I feel connected at a root level with my readers," she suddenly realizes that only one of those proposals will lead her there. She's under no illusions now. She knows which one to choose, and if her editor disagrees, then Nancy knows that she must find a way to take the second idea to a deeper level, too.

As for Lynn, she's facing a different dilemma. While working with a writing partner who has a lot more writing experience than she does, she began to compare her work unfairly and negatively to that person's work. It plunged her into paralyzing self-doubt and wavering. Nancy asked her, "Where do you want your writer's path to lead you, Lynn?" The answer was, "To tell the truth with love and kindness in order to help other people experience life more joyfully." Then Nancy asked her, "Will comparing your work to your friend's work lead to that result?" The answer was obvious. It was one thing for Lynn to learn from her partner, but it was another thing entirely for her to compare herself unfairly. She realized she had not been telling the truth with love and kindness to herself! And she stopped doing that, so that she could continue in the way she chose to go.

Where do you want your path to lead you?

Will this activity or decision or lack of activity lead to that result for you?

When you have answered those questions truly, your wavering will be over, and you will finally be ready to . . . let go.

I developed a writer's block that lasted for nearly nineteen years. I was devastated by a tiny error in my first book. Every time I picked up a pencil, I was afraid of making another mistake.

—Teresa Miller

Letting Go

Step Five on the Writer's Path

•••

You have everything but one thing: madness. A man needs a little madness or else—he never dares cut the rope and be free.
—Nikos Kazantzakis, *Zorba the Greek*

This morning we are ready to enter the mysterious canyon, and start with some anxiety.
—From John Wesley Powell's diary,
reprinted in *Down the Colorado*

You're Tarzan or Jane, swinging from vine to vine in the jungle. You don't release the vine you're holding until you can grab on to a new one, but your hand seems to find the new one before your eyes even see it. You reach, you grasp, it's there, and you swing out into space. You're Superman, shedding Clark Kent's suit and tie in the phone booth. You boldly push off from the pavement, trusting that your red cape will carry you over the pedestrians. You're Lynn, flying down a ski slope while more tentative skiers stand at the top waiting for the perfect time, the perfect path, the right amount of courage. You've worked hard to get to this point, and now you have the skills and confidence to go for it. You're a writer seated in front of an empty page, poised to sail off into unexplored spaces of your imagination.

What do Lynn, superheroes, and some writers have in common?

They have learned how to let go and let their future rise safely up to meet them, whether that future is a mogul, an act of derring-do, or the first word of a poem. They're experiencing a rush of freedom without fear. They are "in their bodies," "in the moment," on a course where going back is no longer an option as they head for experiences they've never known before. Time takes on new dimensions. Paradoxically, by letting go of control, they have become centered and strong and capable. The constraints of ego have melted away, to be replaced by trust, confidence, and vulnerability.

How did they get here? They intentionally took a leap of faith into the unknown because staying where they were was no longer acceptable or because their future called to them so irresistibly. Suddenly, they weren't wavering anymore. They may not even have known why. Their doubts and fears seemed to coalesce into a single hard knot that they could toss behind them. This was it, the do-or-die moment, and they chose to let go.

Letting go is the magic moment when you step off into space, trusting that you won't fall on your face. As the philosopher Søren Kierkegaard said, when we make such a leap of faith, it is the actual act of stepping out that creates a bridge to see us safely to the other side.

It happens throughout all of life, not only in writing.

Some years ago, a novelist we know took this leap of faith. She was on an airplane, feeling sick at heart because she hadn't seen or heard from her runaway son in many years. She didn't know if he was dead or alive, and she had suffered unending agony over the mystery of it. But on that airplane, and without planning to do it, the woman brought an image of him to mind and thought, lovingly and with total conviction, "I release you." Immediately afterward, and although nothing external had changed at all, she felt a peace she had not known since before he left home.

You don't need endless time and perfect conditions. Do it now. Do it today. Do it for twenty minutes and watch your heart start beating.

—Barbara Sher

The next day, her telephone rang. It was her son.

The novelist is convinced it happened because she "let go."

In our experience, most people waver and struggle forever without ever finding the courage and/or inspiration to let go. Many never even reach this go/no-go point because they are held back by fear. But without letting go, you will be limited in your life and in your writing.

The space between here and there can look very empty, very frightening.

Once you've taken that magical step into space, however, a whole new world of writing awaits you. You will have entered a new phase. You can say good-bye to wavering—at least, for now. (It always comes back around, as all the steps do.) But you cannot get there at all without first "letting go" and stepping out into the unknown. And that's what makes this step so difficult, because most people don't want to step into the unknown—at least, not until they've had the experience once in their lives so they know they can survive it. Then they realize that stepping into the unknown and letting go can bring infinite personal rewards.

This Is the Step That Separates Your Future from Your Past

What most inspirational writers and speakers are really talking about is letting go—letting go of old tapes, letting go of fears, letting go of the past and trusting in a future filled with possibilities. If you're like us, when you hear such stories, you are inspired either to think, "Oh, right, that's easy for you to say," or to think that it could happen to you, too.

A poet we know left bankruptcy court one day with less than one hundred dollars to her name. She was seventy years old, with no job, no other source of income, and no one to support her in any way. As you can imagine, she was scared to death, and yet she was surprisingly calm about the bankruptcy itself. She had done everything she knew to try to prevent it, but it had happened anyway. And so on that day in court, she had let go of shame, let go of humiliation, let go of guilt. Letting go in that way gave her peace of mind while she sat there, but it didn't save her assets. She lost everything but her home that day, and she didn't even have the funds to support *it*.

Our friend the poet went home with "her pockets full of empty."

When she walked in the door, there was a message on her answering machine.

"Hi," she heard a cheerful recorded voice say. "We've opened a bed-and-breakfast, and we really want you to come cook for us. Will you do it? We could give you a small salary and free room and board. What do you say?"

What she said later was, "It happened because I let go."

When we let go, we step bravely and unarmed into the future, however dire it looks to us at the time. Then, and perhaps more frequently than we have acknowledged, we are sometimes rewarded with a bit of seeming magic. Help appears where all seemed hopeless. A hand reaches out to save us. An unexpected check arrives. We get an acceptance on a piece of writing, just when it seemed impossible. Many times, what seems to precede that miracle is a combination of acceptance of things as

Before the omelet arrived, I looked at my list of subjects and realized I had accidentally created the table of contents. Now everything I had written had a place to go.

—Lynn Lott

they are, no matter how awful, and then a full letting go—a willing, courageous, and wholehearted surrender to that reality.

Interestingly, it cannot be planned, not any more than coincidences can be planned. In fact, it's a little risky even to speak of it, because it's a mistake to count on it. We don't want to encourage you to do that, although we do encourage you to hold open a place in your heart for unpredictable, uncanny events. But there is no guarantee to this step; there are no rules; there's nothing to predict or to anticipate. There's only the *possibility* that if you can experience the peace of fully letting go, you may receive the gift of what you need the most.

When Nancy was presenting a workshop on this material in Florida, a writer shared his story of letting go. "We were living outside Los Angeles," he said, "and I was commuting to an advertising firm, two hours each way, every day. I hated it. One day, I flew into the house, shouting that I'd had it, I was never going back to that job again, and I was going to find another job, close enough to walk to work. It scared my kids. They wanted to know if we were going to be broke."

He couldn't reassure them. He didn't know what this decision meant for their future; he only knew that he had finally and totally released all of his inner ties to that hated job and commute. "Ten minutes after that," he told them in Florida, "our phone rang. It was a vice president of a public relations firm ten minutes from our house. He said they needed to hire somebody and was there any chance that I'd be interested?" The audience in Florida gasped, but he just smiled and added, "All sorts of magical things like that have happened in my life when I completely let go."

Almost all of the writers we interviewed for this book

spoke glowingly of their own experiences of letting go. Many writers say they experience a letting go whenever they sit down to write, even if they have to prod it a bit to make it happen. For instance, Irene Zabytko creates a letting-go experience for herself by engaging in a ritual a friend taught her about sacred space. She says a special prayer, puts on New Age–ish music, and begins to work. She finds herself letting go, profoundly at peace, even when her writing isn't going well. She feels happy and so lost and absorbed in what she does that, afterward, she is amazed that she has written so much and sometimes even written well. She speaks of this event as mystical and a miracle.

The results of letting go usually do feel miraculous, or magical, to writers.

"Even in my everyday, ordinary writing, letting go feels like magic to me," Nancy says. "How is it that I can sit down to write, knowing only where my scene is set and who is in it to begin with, and then before I know it, characters say things I didn't even know they thought, and they do things I didn't know they could do, and things happen that totally surprise me? How can that be? There's no logical explanation for it or for the sense I get of being in a trance when that happens. There I am, sitting down at my computer, and suddenly, I look up and my senses come flooding back in on me, and I realize I've been writing for two hours without even thinking about it. If that's not magic, then I don't know what is. I think it happens because I give myself over entirely to my writing."

When writers talk about times like that, other people find it eerie.

It is eerie, but it's wonderful to experience, and it doesn't happen without letting go.

You may be disappointed if you fail, but you're doomed if you don't try.

—Beverly Sills

By practicing a lot of "baby let-gos," you build up your courage muscles for the bigger ones. Every time you can let go into your writing, to whatever degree you can, you'll be glad you did, because the rewards are incredible. Writer Cecil Murphey tells what happened recently when he let go: "About two weeks ago, I was working on a book and I must have gone into the 'zone,' because the ringing telephone startled me. I felt as if I had been working in another dimension. At least an hour had elapsed, and yet it had seemed like minutes. When that happens—and it's not an everyday occurrence—the writing feels effortless, and words easily fill the screen."

Another writer, Dan Eckstein, echoes comments we heard from many authors who described this experience in sexual terms, saying that when he lets go, the result feels, "timeless, orgasmic in a life-force manner, awesome to be part of something larger than one's own self, and humble to be a Jedi writer who knows the 'force' is with me."

Sound good? You can reach this kind of release and relief, but beginner, apprentice, or master, first you've got to let go.

All you have to do is look straight and see the road, and when you see it, don't sit looking at it—walk.
—Ayn Rand

Let Go of . . . What?

Boundaries. Old ways of thinking and doing. Fear of failure or success. Self-doubt. Cynicism. Skepticism. Resentment. Defeatism. Old tapes. Neurotic habits. Expectations of any sort, especially the ones that are too high or too low. Outmoded beliefs. Beliefs that hurt you. In his book *In the Zone*, Esalen cofounder Michael Murphy calls letting go a "willingness to give up set responses."

But what does that mean, *set responses*?

In the process of writing this book, there was a moment when we came to an impasse. As Lynn tells it, "I had boxed myself into a corner again and again by a very bad habit that I had created and that I couldn't seem to shake. Simply put, my set response when working on a book was to worry that I might be leaving out something really important. So I'd go through everything I'd ever written to make sure I didn't leave one nugget of gold—not even one bit of gold *dust*—behind. When I first began writing, I didn't have much to go through, so it wasn't a problem. But after twenty-five years of it, I had too much to go through, and yet I felt I had to scour old outlines, articles, books, notes, and so forth, on the chance that I'd find a gem that I had created sometime in the past and had now long forgotten. You can just imagine how long that took! It's easy to see that by following that ritual, I took the fun out of everything."

The most effective way to do it, is to do it.
—Toni Cade Bambara

Then came the new challenge for Lynn.

"Nancy sent me her draft of a chapter I had already worked on, and I couldn't find *me* anywhere in it. So I told her my plan. As usual, I would go back through my version of it and see if she had left out anything that I wanted to salvage."

Lynn didn't get the response she expected from her partner.

"Nancy didn't think I should do that. She suggested that I treat her version as a whole new draft and use it to go on from there. She said, 'Try reading it and judging it as it is, and see if it works. Ask yourself, "Does it feel complete the way it is? Are there holes in it?" If there are, start there. Maybe you'll fill the holes with old material, or maybe you'll be inspired to write something new.'

"But that meant getting my ego out of the way," Lynn says, wryly.

In that instant, Lynn not only got a glimpse of the

mischief she had been causing herself, but she also saw an alternative: don't worry so much that something might be missing that was good in the past; instead, evaluate the present on its own terms and fill in anything that's missing in *it*.

In other words, live in the now in order to create a more original future.

"But could I do that?" she asked herself. "I was ready to start that downhill slide into my *set responses*. Nancy was showing me a new way. But, like Jane the first time she followed Tarzan through the trees, I was terrified to do it, even though I knew it might be a turning point that could kick me into more creativity, joy, and freedom as a writer."

The moment was upon her.

Would she cling to the old vine or let go and grab for the new one? It wouldn't even be as if she were reaching blindly into space, because Nancy had told her how it might be done. She could even see Nancy hanging on to the vine ahead of her, smiling confidently and urging her on. She wanted to follow! The thick, new vine was right there within Lynn's reach, but the space between them looked so scary, and the fall looked so far down. She'd never done this before, and she didn't feel at all confident that she could manage it.

"Nancy had really spit in my soup, if you'll pardon the mixed metaphor," Lynn says. "She made my old way look unpalatable. She kept explaining to me how novelists throw out hundreds of pages, but those pages have to be written in order to get to the better stuff. Once they're done, you don't need to go back to them. She told me how writer friends of hers—Margaret Maron and Judith Greber, for example—never keep their early versions of their chapters. As Judith once said to Nancy, 'I figure that if I rewrote it, I must have thought it needed improving, so why go back to a lesser version?' They literally can't go back and check for what they left out. As you can imagine, it was an appalling idea to me! It made my stomach sink just to think about it. I could hardly believe it was true, that any writer would actually do that, and so Nancy had to explain it to me more than once."

But the gauntlet had been thrown down, the vine was swinging within reach, the phone booth was open for the change of costume, the black-diamond slope was waiting to be skied, the empty page beckoned.

"If I was willing to do as Nancy suggested, I could rid myself of a neurotic pattern that made my life hell *and* I could feel like a 'real' writer, throwing out pages right and left. So what did I do? I conferred with my favorite oracle, the *I Ching*, which said how nice it would be if I didn't go back and how everything should be destroyed behind me! All I would lose, it said, was what I hated and what made me nuts."

She laughs. "I can take a hint."

And so Lynn courageously let go of her old way and tried the new.

"OK, I confess that I took a peek at the draft I had sent to Nancy," she says, "and I'm glad I did, because I saw with my own eyes that Nancy was right and what I had sent looked like drivel even to me." (Nancy wants to emphasize here that all first drafts—especially her own—eventually read like drivel; that's why they're first drafts and not final ones.) "I started anew with a method I now think of as 'riffing.' I gave myself permission to write whatever came to me in any order that it came, and I trusted that it would be the start of something better. So far, I'm having a ball." Riffing has changed her

And if not now, when?
—The Talmud

style and skills as a writer. Now when she's stuck, her husband reminds her to start "riffing" to help her cross over from wavering to letting go.

As Lynn has grown accustomed to swinging through the trees, she has developed her own new way of working that combines remaining open to the "new" with using any old stuff that she wants to put in.

The kind of letting go that Lynn experienced is somewhat related to another kind of letting go that we face whenever we write.

Kill Your Darlings

Have you ever heard the phrase "Kill your darlings?" It means that the phrases, sentences, and so on that we love the best are often the ones we have to edit out, because they call too much attention to themselves. We get too attached to them; we love them too much. In editing our own work, we have to be ruthless. (But better us than an editor or a reviewer.) It's another form of letting go.

"In a book of mine called *Marriage Is Murder*," Nancy recalls, "I originally had a prologue that was twice as long as any other chapter in the manuscript. When I saw that, I realized the book was out of balance; that prologue was too 'heavy' for it; I was going to have to drastically prune it. The problem was, I thought that prologue was the best writing I'd ever done. I had loved writing it so much, more than I had ever enjoyed writing anything else, and I was so proud of it. But it had to be cut, and I made up my mind to do it. I took a deep breath, and then I picked up my pen and started crossing out whole pages. It was painful, at first. But by the time I was halfway through it, I was taking a delicious pleasure in

Hope is putting faith to work when doubting would be easier.

—Anonymous

slicing and dicing it. It ended up being half as long and twice as strong. I threw those precious darlings in the trash and never looked back at them again."

Elmer Williams, author of *Au Revoir Parisienne*, describes one of his cutting experiences: "My writing dream came true when I finally finished a book I had started thirty-four years earlier and got to hold the first copy in my hand," Elmer says. "That was exciting. When I wrote the book, my first draft had 240 pages. I rewrote it about six times with one question in mind: 'Will my reader want to turn to the next page?' I ended up with 128 pages."

Sometimes, we have to sacrifice part of our work in service to the whole.

You Can Want It All, But Can You Have It All?

Sometimes, we have to sacrifice one or more parts of our *life* in service to the rest of it, too. Nancy gave up the job of commercial freelancing in order to dedicate herself to fiction. Other writers have done as much or more. Novelist Lisa Scottoline was a lawyer and a single mom in Philadelphia when she decided to risk it all in the service of becoming a novelist. She left her firm and lived on credit cards, vowing not to stop unless she reached fifty thousand dollars in debt. She reached it. She kept going anyway. When her creditors were sending their third notices and she was afraid she'd risked so much for nothing, her first book sold. She's now a *New York Times* best-selling author and not too worried about practicing law *or* credit-card limits anymore, we hope. We are *not* recommending that just anybody do that! But Lisa is a

I feel there are two people inside of me—me and my intuition. If I go against her, she'll screw me every time, and if I follow her, we get along quite nicely.

—Kim Basinger

dramatic example of somebody who let go of what she had in order to try for what she wanted. People who let go to that degree tend to think that a bird in the hand is *not* worth two in the bush—at least, not if they have a fair chance of grabbing those two.

Emptying the Pitcher

Imagine a pitcher full of water. You want to add fresh water to it. What must you do first? Right. You need to empty some of the old water out to make room for the new. That's the equivalent of letting go. It's also at the heart of one of the principles of feng shui, the ancient Chinese philosophy of harmonious living: empty out the old, dead detritus of your life in order to make room for the fresh and new. It doesn't normally take any courage to pour out some water from a pitcher—or clean out your closet in an exercise of feng shui—but it takes a lot of courage to say good-bye to old ways of living and thinking that don't support your writing.

Letting go means releasing what you don't want in order to try to get what you do want, or letting go of something you want in exchange for something you want more. The reason that's a lot easier said than done is threefold: (1) sometimes, it's really hard to admit exactly what it is you don't want anymore; (2) it can be a challenge to find the courage to let it go; and (3) it's scary to let go without any guarantee that you will ever actually *get* what glitters at you from the other side of the jungle. You could let go . . . and drop like a stone. You could let go and discover the new vine is prickly with thorns, sticky with some disgusting substance, or slippery and hard to grip.

That's the chance we all take when we let go. But we

believe you take a bigger chance when you *don't* let go. More writing doesn't get finished than does. More writing doesn't get published than does. More writers fail than succeed. Those are the odds of writing and of life. It's *because* of those odds that we wrote this book. We believe that doing these steps thoroughly will narrow those odds for you and at the very least make it possible for you to enjoy the process regardless of the outcome of it.

What does it feel like to let go?

Well, think of times in your life when you have done it—at least, to some degree. Do you remember the first time you jumped off a high dive? How about your first ride in a roller coaster? What about when your first child went off to college or to kindergarten? Remember when you signed the contract for your first mortgage or rode a bike or flew in an airplane? It's scary the first time, and sometimes, it continues to be scary. But life is full of letting gos, and every time you experience one, even a tiny one, you strengthen your ability to let go in your writing.

So here's the trick: if you recognize that you are miserly about letting go, if you cling to what you don't need anymore, until your house, your car, your psyche, or your writing is filled with debris, start practicing the fine art of letting go. Start small. Let go of that old coat you haven't worn in years. Let go of that pile of books you'll never read. Don't finish that book you started but aren't enjoying. Let go, let go. Let go of the banister as you walk down the stairs. Let go of the breath you hold when you're nervous. Unclench your hands. Relax your muscles. Let go, let go, let go.

You can't feel the flow until you let go.

Weight Watchers has it down, teaching people to let go of old dieting habits and replace them with new ones

> *What a headlong ride it is! I am soon filled with exhilaration only experienced before in riding a fleet horse over the outstretched prairie.*
>
> —John Wesley Powell

so the pounds can disappear one by one. AA and Al-Anon help people let go one day at a time. Parents let go of their children; children let go of their parents' hands and step out on their own.

How does this translate to your writing?

"The difference between letting go and not letting go in writing," Nancy says, "is like the difference between sitting in the airplane with your parachute on your back and jumping out. It's the difference between clinging to the side of the pool and swimming. It's the difference between following a recipe to the letter or cooking by taste and inspiration. Unless you're a beginning cook, that is, and then letting go may mean simply following a recipe if you've never done it before. It's the difference between the bird who flies around free and the one who never leaves its cage."

Let us say here that we do realize that some "birds," like Emily Dickinson, never leave their "cage" and yet they still manage to produce works of genius. But all you have to do is read Dickinson's poetry to realize that she did let go—inside her head and heart, releasing her imagination to full flight.

For a traditional poet, letting go may mean trying to write in free verse, while for a free-verse poet, it may mean writing sonnets. For a genre novelist, it may mean writing a story with less of a structured plot, while for a literary novelist, it may mean working more with plot. For any kind of writer, it means getting more creative and more true to one's own unique voice.

We know from our own experience that working with a partner is a great way to practice letting go. When Lynn began writing with another of her partners, Jane Nelsen, she'd write a piece in her computer, put it on a

The tape that was playing in my brain said, "You can't make a living as a writer." By 35 I decided I couldn't do anything else better, so I had to do that. I made the step from inspiration to dedication, writing every day without thought of the result, thinking only about the art. It must have worked, because I have an audience of a million people.

—John Lescroart

disk, and give the disk to Jane, who would pop it into her floppy drive, boot it up, and start typing. At first, when Lynn heard those long nails clicking on the keyboard, she cringed, but it didn't take long to learn that Jane made Lynn's work better and Lynn made Jane's work better. They've written two training manuals, four books, and have another book under contract at the time of this writing, and they have done it all by letting go of their separate egos and surrendering into the arena of creativity in which two writers become one brain.

Doing "freewriting" is another great way to practice letting go. Set an alarm clock for ten minutes, then pick a word at random and sit down and write nonstop about that word, saying anything that pops into your mind— without worrying about punctuation, spelling, or anything else—until the alarm sounds. Then put the writing away without looking at it or throw it away, so you won't edit it or judge it. The idea is to set you free from inhibition. "I did this exercise every day for weeks," Nancy says, "when I started fiction full-time. As a former journalist and commercial writer, I was accustomed to telling the truth and to doing it as efficiently as possible. As a fiction writer, I suddenly had to encourage myself to write 'longer,' to unleash my imagination, and to tell lies. It wasn't easy, but I knew that it was essential and that I'd never make it as a storyteller if I couldn't loosen up. Freewriting exercises helped me a lot."

The kind of letting go we're talking about has an end in sight; it's not just risk-taking for the thrill of it, and it's usually not undertaken for the sake of the goal alone. It's undertaken for its own sake, as a show of faith and trust in yourself and your future. You can never guarantee what you will get for doing it, either, because the path on the other side of the bridge rarely looks the way you think it will before you arrive.

When you "freewrite," the end result will be a boost in creativity and your expression of it, but there's no predicting what the exact nature of that will be. When you write with a partner, there's no predicting what the two of you will think up that neither of you could have done alone. When you sit down to write on any given day and let go into your creativity, there is absolutely no telling what will happen next.

Our novelist friend at the beginning of this chapter opened her hand, metaphorically, and let her child have what the child already had anyway—freedom. In so doing, she got peace of mind, and—totally without expecting to—then she got her own child back. Our poet friend opened her hand and let everything she owned go. The next thing she knew, opportunity had landed softly and surprisingly in her open palm. The advertising writer in Florida opened his hand and let unhappiness go, only to find happiness offered to him, shockingly, only ten minutes later.

Just in terms of everyday writing, it may mean that we literally let go of five precious words to get a better sentence. Who knows what that new sentence will be? But it's waiting out there for us, hovering in thin air, invisible until we take the step of letting go of those five precious words. We might let go of five pages to get a better chapter. Or we rewrite so much that by the time we have our four-hundred-page manuscript finished, we've thrown away just as many pages.

Or maybe we let go of everything we've ever done before.

Free-Falling

Nancy once reached a point of letting go in her writing that almost scared her to death. It happened when she was ten years into her fiction-writing career, with several books and many published short stories behind her. Then, when she least expected it, she found herself having a crisis.

"Over a period of a couple of years, I had felt my writing grind to a tedious halt," she says. "I was sick of everything I was writing. The trouble was, I didn't have any idea what could take its place. Nobody had ever warned me this might happen; I mean, does anybody ever warn writers that you can get as tired of writing as teachers do of teaching and plumbers do of plumbing? Who knew? I thought that once you became a published writer, you sat at the pinnacle of happiness for the rest of your life, right? I thought that if you had a mystery series that you loved to write and if it sold pretty well, then you'd be set for life. I thought that I'd always want to write my series and I'd just keep churning them out, and that my publisher would keep printing them and I'd retire on the royalties someday."

What a lovely fantasy. Real life didn't turn out to be like that.

"By the time I started to plot the tenth book in my series, my whole creative spirit was in rebellion, and it couldn't have happened at a worse time. I had a deadline. I had an advance that would only be paid when I handed in the book. I had the mortgage and other financial obligations of any suburbanite. And I had writer's block the size of Utah. I told myself I could force the book out of me by doing the equivalent of a C-section on myself; I could remove that sucker by forceps if I had to.

We know not where we are going. . . . At first this causes us great alarm, but we soon find there is little danger, and that there is a general movement of progression down the river . . . and it is the merry mood of the river to dance through this deep, dark gorge; and right gaily do we join the sport.

—John Wesley Powell

That's what professional writers learn to do. But I hated the idea of doing that. And, professional or no, I wasn't absolutely sure I could do it."

This was more serious than any writer's block she'd ever had before.

"I was having an existential moment, wondering, was I somebody who wrote to pay her bills, or was I really a writer? I truly didn't know anymore. I'd met so many deadlines over the previous twenty-five years that I felt like a skilled craftswoman who could produce a short story or a novel on demand, like a carpenter hired to build a bathroom. I suppose that's a fine thing to be able to do all by itself, but I was hoping for something more meaningful and inspirational in my life than novel-cum-carpentry."

To make matters worse, her father died that year, a romance ended, and all of that exacerbated the identity crisis. She had the feeling that her whole life, not just her career, rode on how she handled this block.

"Well, I have a friend whose motto has always been, 'If it's bad, make it worse until it gets better.' So I decided to allow things to get really bad, if that's what it would take to find out once and for all if I was a 'real' writer. I decided that I wouldn't force myself to finish the book. I wouldn't write until a desire and need to write bubbled up naturally from within me, if it ever did. I was terrified that it never would, because I wasn't sure that I had ever really experienced that in my life, that urge to write that sounds almost like automatic spirit writing when you hear other people talk about it. 'My hand just moved across the paper,' they say.

"That's what I wanted to happen to me. If it didn't—if I just sat there not writing for month after month, this was going to be very bad news, because I had bills to pay and no other means of support. Writing was all I'd ever done as an adult and all I knew how to do. I already knew I was a terrible waitress. Maybe it sounds crazy to say that after thirty years as a professional writer, I had lost faith in my own sense of myself as a writer, but that's how it was. I've since learned this is not an uncommon experience among writers."

And so, one day she committed herself to "not writing" unless the writing itself tugged at her and made her sit down to do it. Then she'd know. If it never happened, she'd know something else. She made the commitment knowing that if the writing didn't come, neither would her income. Scared? Oh, yes, but she swallowed hard and said, "I'm going to do this."

Problem was, she hadn't let go, but she would only know this with hindsight.

Weeks went by, and then months. Her deadline arrived, and she got a postponement. Bills arrived and got paid until there was no more money left to pay them. The next deadline came, and it went by, too. She got asthmalike symptoms, a perfect physical symbol for feeling that what she was writing didn't give her enough creative room to breathe—and that she was suffocating under all of the financial pressure. She became depressed but was afraid to seek medication because she didn't want to mask her feelings or lose her resolve. "I wasn't suicidal," she recalls of that time. "That was my benchmark. If I descended that far, I would know I'd gone *too* far. I longed to be able to talk to people about what I was doing—that's usually the healthy thing to do—but the problem was that I thought I'd only worry them, and they'd try to talk me out of it. It didn't seem right to dump this burden on other people, and I wasn't sure I would be able to withstand their well-meaning negativity.

For he can tell a good story, and is never encumbered by unnecessary scruples in giving to his narratives those embellishments which help to make a story complete.

—John Wesley Powell

What I was attempting to do would look insane and dangerous to them. I would have agreed with them that it was dangerous, but I didn't think it was insane. I doubted, however, that I could make a convincing case for that—at least, not until I succeeded, if I ever did. Thank God, I did open up to one friend, and lucky for me, she understood completely and encouraged rather than discouraged me. She was my lifeline. Not coincidentally, she is also a writer."

Nancy's inner conviction was that she must ride these awful feelings all the way down to the bottom of the well if need be. The problem was, she didn't know what she'd find down there or whether she'd live long enough to make the descent. "There was a day when I felt so ill and had felt so bad for so long that I actually wrote out a list of what my survivors should do after my death. I laugh now to think how melodramatic that sounds, but at the time, that's how bad I felt.

"I was desperate, broke, and sick," she remembers. "I was so frightened of losing everything. And then one day, it all came to a climax. I remember sitting on my couch and realizing that I could still force myself to finish the book. But then, I thought, no, I've come this far with this crazy experiment, I have to go on to the end; I just have to. If I don't, I'll never know, and it will only be worse the next time. I literally sat on my hands that day to prevent myself from forcing the writing out. And then I finally gave up. I wept. I let go entirely. It didn't feel good. It didn't feel like a great relief. But I finally and fully surrendered to whatever might happen."

She went to bed that night feeling utterly defeated and without hope.

That night, she had a dream in which she experienced the same emotions that the heroine in her unfin-

I feel that one must deliberate, then act, must scan every life choice with rational thinking, but then base the decision on whether one's heart will be in it.
—Jean Shinoda Bolen

ished book would feel just at the place where she had stopped writing all those months before. When Nancy woke up, she realized she could never have known those feelings without becoming so scared herself. And then she dared to think, in a kind of whisper of a thought, "Maybe I'll be able to write now."

Hardly daring to breathe, she went into her kitchen, made her morning coffee.

"And then for the first time in my life, I felt a physical sensation of being pulled from my solar plexus. It was the most gentle, subtle tug, but it was there, and it was real. I let it lead me to the couch in my family room; I picked up a pen and paper, and I—who had never written my books or stories on anything but a typewriter or a computer—wrote thirty-six pages in longhand, starting from the place where my book had halted months earlier."

The next day, she wrote twenty-four pages; the next day, twelve; and the next, sixteen; and so it went through page after page of longhand writing, nonstop for two weeks until she finished the book.

"I had never written like that before in my life. It was incredible; it was amazing; it was everything I'd always heard it could be. Mind you, I'm still paying off the debt from that experiment, but I'll never wonder again if I'm a real writer. I know for sure now. It changed forever my way of writing. Now I write all of my stories in longhand first. I'm more creative; I try more interesting and risky things. I care less what other people will think. It freed me in so many ways. It made me a better, more confident, and daring writer. It was one of the hardest things I've ever done. I gave up my financial security and—temporarily—my health to do it, but it was so very worth it."

There were quite a few weekends in a row where I could sit down on a Saturday morning and all of a sudden it was 8 o'clock. Time just disappeared . . . a quantum leap from morning to evening . . . the story just wrote itself.

—Norm Harris

Many letting-go experiences seem to require high risk and prolonged sacrifice of safety or comfort. They require the person to feel extremely uncomfortable for a long time, without drowning those feelings in liquor or sedating them in other ways. If you're going through one of those prolonged periods, it is a blessing to have a friend who has faith when you lose yours, like Nancy's writer friend. (Remember the labor coaches in delivery rooms?) How lucky to have someone around who doesn't scare when you get scared (or who hides it) and who can say with truth, "You can do it. Go for it. Hang in there. Great works don't happen without some pain. You'll make it."

"I've had a longtime editor," Nancy says, "Linda Marrow, who gives her writers that incredible gift of remaining calm when we're not. There have been so many times when I've been struggling with a book, or running late with it, when Linda could have panicked, too, because editors have deadlines, just as we do. But she never, ever has done that. When I'm scared or stuck or worried, her voice is calm and happy and soothing. She makes me laugh. She gives me confidence, by expressing absolutely no doubt in me, ever. Afterward, she'll sometimes admit to having been 'concerned'—which I take as a euphemism for scared shitless—but she understands that worry only weakens the person at whom it's directed and that it's love and faith that help us through. Those kinds of friends, or editors, are like a bridge themselves, allowing you to rest on their support when you're in the toughest parts of your work or your career. May there be a special place in publishing heaven for editors like her and friends like the one who saw me through my toughest challenge."

Think what might have happened if Nancy's friend

had suggested she see a doctor for her condition and the doctor had prescribed antidepressants. Pop open any magazine or think about the commercials you see on your TV. Isn't the message to "not feel"? Or at least not to be uncomfortable? We are convinced that the creative process requires a good bit of discomfort, but we have faith in you to endure and push through it. We think you will feel worse if, instead of letting go, you choose to fall back into the false security of the status quo and live with less than you could have if you let go.

Lynn sees this every day in her therapy practice. Many of her clients would prefer to be diagnosed with an "illness" and take drugs rather than do the work of living, taking the necessary risks required to ensure growth instead of a slow death. But if they stick it out as Nancy did, they learn how to let go, feel the release, and enjoy the ride.

How Do You Let Go?

Lynn's favorite way to help her clients let go is to introduce them to what she calls *top cards*. A top card is a behavior that comes to the surface in a crisis. It's a "set response," in other words. Therapy clients aren't the only ones who have them—we all do.

There are four top cards: control, superiority, pleasing, and comfort.

To help her clients understand them, Lynn compares them to the behaviors of certain animals—the eagle, the lion, the chameleon, and the turtle. She even has a basket filled with stuffed animals to represent each of the four top cards. It seems that it is easier for clients to visualize animals being defensive and holding on tight than it is to see themselves as too scared to try something new.

If you're never scared or embarrassed or hurt, it means you never take any chances.

—Julia Sorel

Lynn suggests that her clients think about what a turtle, an eagle, a chameleon, or a lion might do when faced with a threat. For most people, the idea of letting go is definitely a threat. When she asks that question of her clients, they tend to say that the turtle will hide in its shell or snap, the eagle will fly to its nest, the chameleon will change colors and try to blend in, and the lion will roar or attack. To which Lynn replies to her clients, "That's probably what you do, too." As do we all. "We can display any of those behaviors," Lynn continues, "but there's usually one that each of us leads with, just like laying down a card in bridge or poker."

It's natural at this point for clients to want to find out which animal they are, and perhaps you would like to discover your animal, too. If so, here's a simple way to do it. All you have to do is look at the four boxes in the accompanying illustration and *pick the one that has in it what you most would like to avoid dealing with*. Go with your first instinct and don't think too hard.

If you chose the box with stress and pain, it tells you that your top card is comfort. You are like a turtle when you get scared to let go, and so you may retreat even further into your shell and snap at anybody who tries to draw you out of it. Real-life turtles say that when they feel stressed, they eat or procrastinate and wish others would simply empathize with them.

If you chose the box with criticism and ridicule, your top card is control. You act like an eagle when you feel afraid to let go, flying into a rage, squawking, and flapping your wings if you think someone caught you doing something stupid. We've watched eagles behave this way when trapped for banding at the Hawk Watch blind in the Florida Keys. They do not take nicely to being caught. Real-life eagles said that when they are stressed, they organize, shut down, work frantically, argue and explain, and get defensive. What they are wishing for in that moment is acceptance and understanding, not an easy thing for other people to give them, what with those talons curling and those wings flapping.

If you chose rejection and hassles, your top card is pleasing, and you are like the chameleon when you're fretting about letting go. Your survival instinct tells you to blend in, keep quiet, look cute, and try not to get your tail cut off. Real-life chameleons aren't really sure what they do, but they know how they *feel* when stressed— overwhelmed, guilty, defeated, compromised, and anxious. They are hoping that someone will understand what they are going through, put it in perspective, and say, "I wish I were just like you."

If you chose the box with meaninglessness and unimportance in it, your top card is superiority, and you become a lion when threatened by the idea of letting go. In that case, you may hide out in your cave doing absolutely nothing or go on the attack, ripping your perceived threat to bloody shreds. Real-life lions say that when

Action may not always be happiness but there is no happiness without action.
—Benjamin Disraeli

they are stressed, they cry, scream, complain, criticize, catastrophize, and blame. What they need is for you to submit or understand or appreciate them or nourish and cheer them on. You can imagine how hard it would be to give these people the help they need when they are playing their top card, because their survival behaviors are pretty scary.

To see how it works, let's start with Nancy's top card, comfort, for a closer look.

Nancy didn't get anybody's permission to run her "experiment" with creativity, as someone with an eagle top card might have done. She would have liked to have got the confirmation and support of family and friends, as a chameleon might need, but when she didn't think she'd get it, she went ahead anyway. And she didn't do it because she thought she'd change the world, as a lion might, although she did have a sense that maybe she was doing a small but important thing. No, she did it because she was so uncomfortable being the writer she was that she had to find another, more comfortable way to work, even if it meant feeling incredibly uncomfortable in the process. (Here, finally, is the answer to the old joke, Why did the turtle cross the road? Because she thought it just had to be more comfortable on the other side!)

Top-Card Writers in Action

If you're a turtle like Nancy who has a comfort top card, you'll know that you probably won't let go unless you allow yourself to get so uncomfortable with your present circumstances that you just can't stand it anymore. Do trust your gut and do what feels best to you, but if you want to speed up the process a bit, try taking any small step you can to "just do it." Then take the next small step and then the next and then the next. Things tend to look bigger to turtles than they really are, sometimes. Also, look for people who are empathetic and who don't give you advice or try to fix things for you, and you'll be well on your way to release and relief. Turtles need cheerleaders, not advice columnists. It can be very scary to cross that highway all alone, but all you really need is somebody at the side of the road to scream if they see a truck bearing down on you or to cheer you on.

If you're a writer with a control top card (eagle), you come equipped with an ability to manage crisis, so letting go may not seem so difficult—if the person doing it is someone else. What a great opportunity for you to jump in and manage someone else's messes. But when it comes to letting go of something personal, that's another story, especially if it means the possibility of suffering humiliation or criticism. Then you feel you must cover all the bases first, and then just for good luck, re-cover them before taking a risk. You can stay stuck in this base-covering endeavor (that looks like procrastination) until someone you trust gives you permission to do what you want instead or points out options you didn't see. When you know you have choices or permission, you can fly like the eagle, gliding freely on the thermals.

People with an eagle top card might not like it if we mention their names, but we could tell a story or two of what works and what doesn't for them. Being an employee or a contract writer seems to be ideal, for instance, while living on royalties is not. As a writer-for-hire, the risk factor for making money is minimized; the boss/contractor/publisher gives the map of what is wanted, so the bases are already covered; and if the material is controversial or uninteresting, the criticism goes to the person who's paying the bills instead of to the author.

You can have faith in writing itself. That's where to place your faith, in the same way that a pole vaulter places his faith in the laws of physics. He will go up in direct proportion to the strength with which he pushed off, and he will come down every time.

—Nancy Pickard

For an eagle, there's a tremendous freedom and release in being given permission to write your way and get paid for it, without any additional risk.

For writers with pleasing top cards to feel secure enough to let go, they need confirmation that they are doing the right thing. Chameleons may think they are being exceptionally clever and brilliant, but they're not quite sure, so they spend a lot of time looking for approval. When they get it, life is grand, and when they don't, God help the person who isn't pleased with them.

Lynn has a pleasing top card, which is why she needed Nancy to keep telling her it was OK to stop working her old way and to try something new. Since folks with this top card are chameleons, it also makes sense that while Lynn worked with Nancy, she adapted herself to the way her new partner worked, much more so than Nancy the turtle adapted herself to Lynn. For instance, she didn't take the laptop on their first working trip, even though she knew Lynn was expecting her to. For various reasons, it wouldn't have felt comfortable to the turtle to do that, so she stubbornly didn't. (The fact that Nancy's a turtle also helps explain the fact that she can write literally anywhere, since turtles carry their shells on their backs. Lynn the chameleon, on the other hand, has to be where she has at least a fighting chance of blending in naturally with her environment. If she can't, she's so uncomfortable, she has a hard time working. Eagles are happy working on multiple projects at once, especially for other people, and they can work in the middle of the freeway and feel right at home, while lions love best to work in one of two extremes: everything is perfectly organized, or everything is cluttered chaos. You can spot a lion by the desktop with only a pen

Have you had an orgasm lately, because if you have, that's what letting go feels like.

—Anonymous

and piece of paper on it or a desk that looks as if it belonged to Walter Matthau in *The Odd Couple*.)

If you are a writer with a superiority top card, a lion, you need to think your actions can change the world. You might have a hard time letting go of what seems to be the one and only right way to do things—at least, according to you. Your black-and-white thinking limits possibilities, however, and the thought of looking stupid or not being perfect can be a big deterrent to letting go. "I hate to look foolish" is a common theme with proud lions. But if it appears that someone else is moving ahead faster or that further growth won't happen without new ideas, you'll get what you're after, moving with speed and overtaking your prey, kind of like a lion.

Jane Nelsen is a writer with a superiority top card. One year, Jane wrote or rewrote ten books, all of which have life-changing potential for the readers. And did she love the pace? Yes. The challenge of doing more than anyone should or could do is freeing for her, as it is for most lions. Jane's books can change how people parent their children, affecting future generations for years, and what more can a person with this top card ask for than that? Fame? Money? That usually comes with their territory. After all, they are king and *queen* of the jungle.

Lucky for you, you have even more options than the animals do. If you only do what you are used to doing to protect yourself—if you keep playing out your top card in a knee-jerk kind of way, that is—nothing will change and letting go will be impossible. Turtles will keep retreating and delaying their own movement forward. Eagles will insist on so much control that they can't possibly relax and let go. Chameleons will never say no to other people and yes to themselves. And lions will be all big talk and no action. Playing a top card is a protective move, but the only thing it protects is the status quo. If you are happy with the status quo, that's fine. But if you are so happy with it, then what are you doing at this step, poised at the edge of letting go?

Your top card, played out without thinking, only keeps you right where you are, even when it's time for you to go on and even when you don't like where you are. Worse yet, you almost always end up with what you were trying to avoid in the first place. So the turtle suffers pain and stress by trying to avoid it, the eagle ends up with the criticism and ridicule he hates, the chameleon ends up feeling rejected and unloved, and the lion ends up feeling as if all she has ever done is work so that her family might eat.

Want to Try Something New?

Don't worry, we're not trying to take your security blanket away from you. You can always do your old behaviors; they'll still be around if you need them. But if you're ready to let go and make a change, here are new behaviors you can practice. If you are a turtle, try telling somebody what's going on with you, and tell him everything. No hiding, no secrets, no protecting yourself from what he might think, say, or do. If you don't want opinions or fixing, let the person to whom you are talking know that all you need is empathy. Once you have that, you can trust your gut and move forward step by step to the other side of the road, where it is almost sure to feel more comfortable for you.

If you're an eagle, try writing what you feel like writing anytime you feel like it, instead of writing things only in a "proper" order. Try freewriting: write as fast as you can for ten minutes a day with no regard for punctuation, spelling, anything but getting the words down without thinking. If you are still stuck, talk over your dilemma with somebody who has, in your opinion, enough authority to give you the permission to want what you want and to go for it. And know that being a writer comes with lots of criticism for everyone who tries it, so if criticism comes your way, you don't have to take it so personally. Just consider it a badge of being in the "writers' club."

If you're a chameleon like Lynn, ask someone you admire to confirm for you the rightness of what you want to do. Don't be afraid to speak up because you might look stupid or your ideas may be rejected. And if you don't agree with someone or like what she is asking, speak up! Your opinions do count. As for being so thin-skinned, does the expression "try again" have any meaning for you? It should, because in the real world, a chameleon can grow back a tail that's been severed. And don't forget that it is *not* your job to keep everybody happy. Practice the word *no* a few dozen times a day.

As for you perfectionist lion writers, don't let your quest for perfection paralyze you. There's no perfect antelope out there. There's no perfect writing, perfect writing time or space, perfect review, perfect agent, editor, publisher, or anything else. Instead, concentrate on putting enough meaning and significance into what you want to do, because that's what's really important to you. The quest for perfection in superficial things is merely a cover for the more important quest for meaning that guides your inner life. It doesn't hurt to check things out, either, although it may bruise your pride to admit you need to. Like a lion, you may be so used to thinking

*Letting go
is . . .
twirling,
spinning,
jumping,
sliding,
diving,
dancing.*

—Lynn Lott

you are the only one who knows anything and you have all the right and best answers that you may be surprised to find out just how much others have to offer if you give them a chance. When you have let go, and you are in the Immersion step, revel in the opportunity to discover that there are many ways to do the same thing. You are looking for the one that resonates for you.

Here's something else that's useful about learning to recognize when you are playing your top card and acting like an animal. Once you recognize those signs in yourself, you can then ask yourself, "What am I afraid of? What is the worst thing that could happen? Can I handle it? If I can't, do I know someone who has a different top card/perspective, and could I ask that person what he or she would do in the same situation?"

Every time you face your fears, acknowledge them, and try a behavior outside of your comfort zone, you strengthen your letting-go muscle. Like any other muscle, the stronger it is, the better it works and the freer you'll feel as a person and a writer.

Get Ready to Fly!

The kind of letting go we have been talking about is a character-building experience. Why wouldn't writers want to let go? What could stop them from experiencing the joy that comes from free-flowing writing? Why wouldn't they want to feel free, exhilarated, light, unencumbered, and relieved? How could they pass up a high that they wish would last forever or a sense of power that comes from their work? Who wouldn't want to be in their body, doing what they are meant to do, working creatively, magically, with no worry about the outcome? This is the step you must take before you get the opportunity to "flow" with your writing. It's all about saying good-bye to your past and saying hello to your future in a magical present moment. So grab that vine, shed that business suit, fly down that ski slope, face that blank page, and let go into a richer, deeper writing life.

The bridge will rise up to meet you and carry you to the next step on this path, where you will join the lucky company of writers who are immersed in their work.

Immersion

Step Six on the Writer's Path

• •

*Once in his room he resumed his writing. The days and nights
came and went, and he sat at his table and wrote on. He went
nowhere, save to the pawnbroker, took no exercise, and ate
methodically when he was hungry and had something to cook,
and just as methodically went without when he had nothing
to cook. . . . He worked on in a daze, strangely detached from
the world around him.*

—Jack London, *Martin Eden*

*There were quite a few weekends in a row where I could sit
down on a Saturday morning and all of a sudden it was eight
o'clock at night. Time just disappeared . . . a quantum leap
from morning to evening . . . and the story just wrote itself.
I've had that happen quite a few times.*

—Norm Harris

*Once I've settled in, I barely notice time passing. I'm as happy
as a mortal creature can be.*

—Nina Osier

Here is your reward at last, the reason you started on this
path in the first place.

This is the payoff step, much more so for most writers
than even the final step is, because if the writing itself doesn't satisfy

you, it's unlikely that the completion of it will. As Toni Morrison has said, "Struggling through the work is extremely important—more important to me than publishing it."

This is the step in which you finally get to do the work you've longed to do, the work that made you feel so unhappy *not* to be doing it, the work to which you have committed yourself. "I can't tear myself away," says writer Barbara Seranella of the times when she's immersed in her writing. "I walk about with a Cheshire cat smile, and I want to tell everyone how brilliant I am." And no wonder! By this step, you've faced the worst of your doubts and fears. You've let go of all of that as much as you possibly can, and now you finally get the chance to do the work itself, the writing.

Congratulations are very much in order.

You've earned this. You've come a long, long way to reach this step.

Has it been worth it? Ultimately, only you can tell, but we could quote thousands of writers who'd all tell you that it's been worth it to them, just to get to experience this step. Listen to Steve Dixon extol the joy of being immersed in his writing: "Somehow, I plugged in to that other universe, the universe where the stories live. I became a channel for the stories. I simply acted as the channel for the energy of the stories to flow through me. It was like sexual energy flowing through me to my lover. It was ecstatic. And I could do it for hours and hours."

"The most interesting thing about writing," claims Gore Vidal, "is the way it obliterates time. Three hours seem like three minutes."

"I think it's like when you're hungry," is writer Eric

My gratitude for good writing is unbounded; I'm grateful for it the way I'm grateful for the ocean.

—Anne Lamott

Burton's description of it, "when you crave something to eat. There is anticipation, your mouth waters, you can almost taste the food. Seconds feel like minutes, minutes feel like hours, and finally, there it is right in front of you! The taste is everything you expected, and better. That's how I feel when I'm immersed in my writing. I get exhilarated every time I sit down to write. My words appear on the screen, and the story takes on its own life. That is when the adrenaline rush comes. For me, the exhilaration, the adrenaline, and the freedom are all there from the moment I sit down and begin to write."

As novelist Elmer Williams sums up, "When the thoughts come faster than you can put them down, it gets pretty exciting!"

These periods can last for a few blissful minutes, or they can go on for a very long time. In her novel *Ring of Truth*, Nancy's heroine, who is also a writer, describes the aftermath of finishing a book:

> So many phone calls left unanswered. So many letters unopened, bills unpaid, so much E-mail ignored. I wonder if I missed any appointments. Probably. I think I paid the mortgage for this month, but I'm not sure.

A little later, she says:

> I look around my office, as if seeing it for the first time since I launched this final push to the end of the book, and what I see through critical eyes is a disaster area. Books and papers piled everywhere. Old food crusting on plates. Coffee cups with milky sludge. And what's my brassiere doing over there, draped across that footstool? I must have taken it off on my way to the shower one night and never noticed it again until this moment.

Sometimes, but certainly not every time, the quality of those chapters amazes me. I'll read three or four pages and say to myself, "I don't remember writing that." They're my words and my style, so I know my fingers tapped out those sentences, but it's as if I had gone into another dimension during the process.

—Cecil Murphey

What's a messy house compared to days of nonstop writing?

Of course, that's when the writing is going well.

Sometimes, many times, it doesn't go well at all, and that's why this is a two-part step, consisting of both *resolve* and *preoccupation*. It's only by maintaining your resolution to write that you even get the chance to experience the bliss of being so preoccupied with your writing that time disappears.

"I'm not sure I understand the process of writing," novelist Elizabeth Hardwick admits. "There is, I'm sure, something strange about imaginative concentration. The brain slowly begins to function in a different way to make mysterious connections. Say it is Monday, and you write a very bad draft, but if you keep on trying, on Friday, words, phrases, appear almost unexpectedly. I don't know why you can't do it on Monday, or why I can't. I'm the same person, no smarter, I have nothing more at hand."

Nothing at hand, that is, except her resolve to keep writing.

"In the end, a man must sit down and get the words on paper, and against great odds," E. B. White wrote. "This takes stamina and resolution. Having got them on paper, he must still have the discipline to discard them if they fail to measure up; he must view them with a jaundiced eye and do the whole thing over as many times as is necessary to achieve excellence, or as close to excellence as he can get."

That's resolve.

The other half of this step—being *preoccupied* with your writing—is a result of resolve and often seems so easy and joyous that it hardly feels like working. When Nina Osier said at the start of this chapter that immersion

Happiness consists in the full employment of our faculties in some pursuit.

—Harriet Martineau

makes her feel "as happy as a mortal creature can be," she also added, "even when (this may sound strange) the book is driving me nuts right then."

Most writers will get to enjoy at least some of those moments of blissed-out preoccupation. But it's the first part of this step—being *resolved* to remain true to your work even when it gets hard—that separates the real writers from those who only dream of writing. Writers *are* dreamers, of course, but as Goethe said, "In the realm of ideas, everything depends on enthusiasm; in the real world, all rests on perseverance." In his book *On Writing*, Stephen King put it a lot more bluntly: "Sometimes you have to go on when you don't feel like it, and sometimes you're doing good work when it feels like all you're managing to do is shovel shit from a sitting position."

Whether you feel as if you're going with the flow or shoveling shit from a sitting position, Immersion is the realm of those extremes and everything in between. This is the step in which the work gets done; this is the realm of enthusiasm and perseverance; this is the step of preoccupation and resolve.

Nancy says she knows a lot of writers who never get past the middle of a book, or they never do the rewrites, or they give up at the first hint of criticism or the tenth rejection. Sometimes, for some people, that's the appropriate thing to do. Maybe the book was a bad idea to start with, or they're not ready to write it. Or maybe they're not old enough or mature enough yet to be able to be critiqued without feeling destroyed. Or maybe there's truly no market for what they're writing. There are lots of legitimate reasons to quit.

But sometimes, Nancy wonders if maybe they don't

There are half hours that dilate to the importance of centuries.

—Mary Catherwood

understand that it gets hard—because it is hard. This is the step that people tend to underestimate the most. They don't understand that, on the whole, and in spite of those moments of bliss, writing is damned hard work for most of us. Getting published is even harder. Sticking with a writing project or a writing career is *really* hard. This is not an easy job, but it looks easy to people who don't know anything about it.

She tells a story that will sound familiar to professional writers.

"Once a pompous ass of a surgeon said to me that he knew he could write a novel if he just had the time. Later, I wished I had said to him, 'Yeah, you could write a novel like I could do surgery. We could both probably handle the beginning and the ending. It's the middle we'd muddle.' "

People like that tend to think that any fool can write, or else why would they think *they* could? But the truth is that even the most humble and modest of beginners tend to underestimate what it takes to be a writer. So then, when they come up against the hard parts—and there are *always* hard parts—they're shocked, hurt, confused, and too easily discouraged.

The people around you will come up against the hard parts of your writing life, too, we guarantee it.

"A friend of mine called one day," Lynn remembers, "and asked me if she could spend four days with my husband and me at our home in the mountains. I told her I'd love that, and that I could be free to play with her after 3:00 P.M. each day when I was finished with my writing. She didn't understand that. She said, with surprise and disapproval in her voice, 'You don't work on Saturdays, do you?' I told her, yes, I do. I see clients in

My parents have been visiting me for a few days. I just dropped them off at the airport. They leave tomorrow.

—Margaret Smith

I can't understand writers who feel they shouldn't have to do any of the ordinary things of life, because I think that this is necessary: one has to keep in touch with that. . . . The ordinary action of taking a dress down to the dry cleaner's or spraying some plants infected with greenfly is a very sane and good thing to do. It brings one back, so to speak. It also brings the world back.

—Nadine Gordimer

my counseling practice all week, so my only time to write is the weekends, and that's sacred time to me. So then she tried bargaining with me. 'Well, how about Sunday?' she asked me, and then she kind of whined, 'Can't you at least take Sunday off?' I told her no, and all the while, I was thinking, 'Welcome to the writing life.' I did what I could, though, to make things better for her. I said, 'I know you can find lots to do without me. You're welcome to our car, the bikes, the raft, anything we've got. But you'll just have to pretend I'm not here while I'm writing.' She wasn't happy with that and decided not to come at all if I couldn't spend the amount of time with her that she wanted to spend with me. I was really sorry she didn't come, but I knew I'd be a whole lot sorrier if I didn't stick to my guns and write."

An important part of resolve is being loyal to yourself and your work.

To quote Stephen King again, "Come to it [writing] any way but lightly. Let me say it again: *you must not come lightly to the blank page.*"

We think it's important for writers to understand what he meant by that or at least what it means to us when we read it. It doesn't mean you can't write "funny." It doesn't mean you can't write sweet or light-hearted things. It doesn't mean you can't approach your notebook or laptop with a soaring, joyous heart. Not at all. It doesn't mean you have to be dreadfully somber or take yourself seriously all the time. It may be *War and Peace* you're doing, but it's not actual war, after all. Mystery writer and longtime *Writer's Digest* fiction columnist Lawrence Block tells the story of how he used to keep himself from getting intimidated or taking himself too seriously by posting a sign near his typewriter: "IT'S JUST A BOOK."

To us, what Stephen King said means—be loyal to your writing. Be just as loyal as you are to your dearest friend or loved one. If your friend or your child really needed your attention, would you let your attention wander? Or would you ignore the telephone, put everything else on hold, and turn fully toward him or her? Your writing deserves that kind of loyalty and attention, too. If you can't or won't manage to show as much loyalty to your writing as you show to your friends and family, we guarantee that while you may experience moments of writing bliss, you'll never experience the satisfaction of going all the way.

Be loyal. "Don't live with a lover or roommate who doesn't respect your work," says the short-story writer Grace Paley. "Buy time to write if you have to," she goes on to say. In fact, "borrow to buy time," if you have to. Do anything, in other words, to make it possible for yourself to write. "Write what will stop your breath if you don't write," Paley says. In other words, if you privately think, "I'll die if I can't write," that may just be true. And so the ultimate loyalty to yourself is to write in order to save your life.

In exchange for your life, know that your writing will ask a lot of you. It will drive a hard bargain. Writing asks a lot of all of us who do it, as does any art or anything worth doing. Be prepared to give it what it requires. Know that it's going to be hard to persevere sometimes.

Don't make the mistake of thinking it's a lark to be a writer, because it isn't. Sure, there are many pleasures to be had from the writing life, but no more than from any other loved job done well. And besides, even "larks" have to work hard to build their nests, you know, to feed their families, to survive, and that's no less true of writers.

In this step, you can experience moments of preoccupation without showing much resolve, but they won't last long or do you much good in the long run. It's *resolve* that gives backbone and discipline to your writing life so that you can stay with it for the long haul. It's resolve that makes it possible for you to be preoccupied with your writing as much as it needs for you to be.

Since resolve is hard, let's talk about it some more.

Be It Resolved: That I Write

Resolve is an interesting word, different from *commitment* in a significant way. According to *The Random House Dictionary of the English Language*, *commitment* means the act of pledging or engaging oneself, as you would to a fiancé. "Will you marry me?" "Yes, I will marry you." That's a clear commitment, but it's not a marriage. "Will you write a poem?" "Yes, I will write a poem." That's a commitment, but it's not a poem. "Will you quit your job and write full-time?" "Yes, I will write full-time." That's a hell of a commitment, but it's still only words.

Resolve, on the other hand, means to make up your mind to follow a course of action; it is marked by will and a firmness of purpose. "Do you take this woman to be your lawfully wedded wife?" "I do." That's resolve, the real thing, a much more serious business than a commitment. "Do you write every day?" "I do." No more promises now; this is the step in which you begin to marshal your want power to go along with your intent. This is where you bring forth continued and steady effort, not just wishes and hopes. This is the step of applying the seat of your pants to the seat of your chair.

Interestingly, in the dictionary, neither of our two words, *commitment* and *resolve*, is used to define the other.

Commitment is definitely different from resolve, therefore, and it's exactly like the difference between an engagement and a marriage. Up until now, you've just been engaged to write; now it's time to take the vow to live together with your computer until death do you part. Or at least, to work on that article, book, story, or poem until it's finished!

Commitment is about saying you'll do something; resolve is about doing it.

> Build a little
> fence of trust
> Around today;
> Fill the space with
> loving work,
> And therein stay.
>
> —Mary
> Frances Butts

A Constant Test of Your Resolve

The actual work of writing is an almost constant test of that resolve.

Nina Osier tells about how, "last winter, as I wrote the second draft of *Starship Castaways* (after throwing the first draft in the trash can four months earlier and then having surgery—not a nice autumn at all!) . . . I sat at my keyboard and the story finished itself as if it were downloading through my hands. That's where I get the 'rush,' when the characters take over and all I have to do is—record them."

Sounds easy, doesn't it?

But please carefully examine what she said, and note what she did: this was her *second* draft of a novel that she was talking about. And she sat down to work on it after apparently being so disappointed in her first draft that she literally threw it away and after a four-month hiatus in which she had surgery. And still, she returned to her computer. And still, she sat down to write. Nina remained loyal to her ideas, to herself, to her book, to her writing. That takes *resolve*. And *that's* how you get to the "flow."

You can't feel the magic of total immersion in your writing if you don't first sit down to do the work. When Nina sat down that first day back at her computer, she didn't know what would happen. Hell, it had been four months since she'd worked on the damned thing! For all she knew, the whole idea could have died in the meantime. She'd been through a lot already. She could have given up. She could have done anything but what she actually did, which was to sit down at her computer, put her hands on the keyboard, and wait to see what would happen next.

So many, many things will tempt you, distract you, and try to lure you away from showing your resolve.

"Every little interruption," Nora Roberts reports, "—a phone ringing, a dog whining to go out, a husband lurking somewhere in the house—is an itch under the skin. Which goes to my opinion that anyone who marries a writer deserves to be pitied."

It's almost as if writing is your spouse and everything *else* is the tempter beckoning its finger at you: *"Oh, don't write today. Come and be with me, instead."* The tempter can take millions of different forms, ranging from the beauty of a summer day to the summons of dirty laundry. It can take the form of people who would find other things for you to do, or it could take the form of emotional problems such as depression and anxiety. It can be money worries or laziness, procrastination or perfectionism. It can be as many distractions as there are words in the dictionary. And more. Put a kaleidoscope up to your eye and turn the dial and keep on turning it forever: in the infinitely changing patterns, you can see symbolized

The medals don't mean anything and the glory doesn't last. It's all about your happiness. The rewards are going to come, but my happiness is just loving the sport and having fun performing.

—Jackie Joyner-Kersee

all of the varieties of things that can tempt you away from writing, that stand in the way of your writing, or that push you away from your writing if you let them.

But you're going to be loyal, remember?

That's why Lynn takes herself and her writing as far away from distractions as she can get. "My husband can be immersed in something with a roomful of people around," she says. "He is able to do the project in his head and shut out the rest of the world. Sometimes, I look at him, and although I see his body, I know no one's home inside of it. He's off on some mental trip to some land that is completely his. Oh, to have that level of concentration!"

She doesn't have that, she says.

"I've had a fantasy since I was a kid watching that old TV show *The Millionaire*, in which million-dollar checks were handed out to people to spend as they pleased. Only, in *my* fantasy show, you only get the money if you agree to live without human contact for a whole year. I fantasize about trying that, but I know me. It would start out just fine. I'd hole up for a year in a cottage without a phone, seeing no one, being alone, and figuring out what I'd really do with all that time. But the truth is, I'd probably install a phone line for my E-mail, and before you know it, I'd be inviting people over for a visit. Yikes! I have a hard time saying no to lunches I don't really want to go to, saying no to skiing with friends on days when I'd rather be writing, inviting people to dinner because 'it's been too long,' or just filling my spare time with errands instead of with writing. That's my basic personality—I tend to try to please other people and let my own needs slide."

Remember in step two when we showed how your

For me the process works best with no interruption, no breaks in the steady application, no letters to be answered, very little social life, no holidays; it is therefore a form of happy imprisonment.

—Patrick O'Brian

body always tells the truth about what you really want? In her case, Lynn's body repeatedly tells her—whether she likes to hear this news or not—that what she apparently wants most is to please other people, even if that means sacrificing her own time to write. "That's the biggest obstacle to my writing," she admits. "It's my fear that people won't be happy, or they'll feel ignored or unloved or think I'm selfish and uncaring." She wants to please them, partly for their sakes and partly for her own.

But she also really wants to write.

The two "wants" frequently conflict in her life.

For a long time, Lynn thought there was only one way to solve that conundrum. She let herself be used up by other people until it got so extreme that she felt absolutely driven to start saying no and to write again, but this way had obvious disadvantages. One was that "when the pile got too big, I didn't know where to start. Then it seemed that no matter what I did, I'd end up running out of time, so why even bother starting? When I felt that way, I knew that the only thing to do was to pick up the first piece of paper, deal with it, and then pick up the next one and deal with it, and so on, until I got some momentum going. When I was overwhelmed by all the writing I had to do, seemingly without enough time to do it, I would set a timer and tell myself to see what I could do in ten minutes or fifteen or an hour and get started that way."

The only thing that makes one place more attractive to me than another is the quantity of heart I find in it.
—Jane Welsh Carlyle

Those ways worked, but they weren't how she wanted to live.

"When I'm whining about not having enough time, I am at the depth of my discouragement," Lynn knows. "At those times, I have no good energy for writing. I get stuck on the horns of my own dilemma, my way of looking at my world as either/or. I start thinking, I can either have enough time to write or I can have enough time to earn a living with my counseling practice, but if I do the one, I'll starve, and if I do the other, I'll feel exhausted and cheated out of my enjoyment in my writing. In my childlike way, I create two choices, when the truth is that the world holds millions of choices if I could only see them."

When she gets in fixes like that, she thinks of something Anton Chekhov is reputed to have said: "My country house is full of people, they never leave me alone; if only they would go away I could be a good writer." It comforts her to know that even Chekhov had trouble saying no. But it doesn't solve her basic problem, any more than it probably solved his.

She has learned another way—to remove herself from temptation.

When she does so, she's not trying to change her basic personality, and she's not caving in to its weaker moments. Instead, she's working *with* it in order to enable her writing.

"The truth about me," she says, "is that I'm like the princess in the story of the princess and the pea. Every little noise or distraction bothers me. That's why I hide out at our home in the mountains, or I leave town and rent a place for a week to give myself the privacy I need and love for my writing."

But what if you're easily distracted like Lynn, but you can't afford to get away?

"Recently," Lynn says, "we rearranged our home so I could have a separate room with a door for my writing space. And it's not just any room, either, but one with a

Nothing is work unless you'd rather be doing something else.

—George Halas

lot of light and greenery outside my window, because I really love to feel as if I'm in the woods when I'm writing, even if I'm inside."

And if that kind of rearrangement isn't possible for you, either?

Rob and Trish MacGregor, both full-time writers, created a writing space for him by turning their dining room into an office and building "walls" out of bookcases. Even then, it was hardly private, since it was a "through" room to the rest of the house, but it was the best they could do with the space they had, and it must have worked OK, because Rob wrote twelve books there.

For years, Nancy wrote in an office in her basement. It wasn't pretty, it was damp, it had no windows, but people had to think twice before descending the stairs to bother her down there. (After she told this to a group of first graders years ago, one little boy asked her, "Does your husband ever let you come up out of the basement?") Another time, she borrowed an empty office from friends who owned an apartment building. There was spare office furniture piled up all around her, but she had complete privacy, and all she had to pay was the utilities.

And if you can't even find a corner in a basement?

"Here's the rub," Lynn says. "We may have a picture of the ideal writing situation, and that gets in the way of how things really are in our lives. My fantasy is that I make a decision to sit down and write and then I just do it—in a perfect office with perfect scenery right outside the windows. Nobody bothers me. The air is fresh. I feel great. I'm engaged, engrossed, focused, connected, passionate, and productive. The writing goes beautifully. At the end of the time allotted, I look up, notice the time

Every day we have to produce the best Wall Street has to offer. We just start writing. We don't sit down and start thinking.

—Tom Dorsey, CNBC Stock Analyst

has passed, the project is finished, and it's done perfectly with no glitches. Need I say that it's not like that most of the time?"

Even so, she creates the best environments she can. Sometimes, she can't get to that perfect writing idyll she has in the mountains, but she writes anyway. Sometimes, the world won't stay outside that closed door of her writing room at home, but she writes anyway.

You do what you can; you do what you have to do to keep writing.

Nancy has written in her car in parking lots, under trees beside soccer fields, in a rose garden, at a zoo. She has written in school car-pool lanes; she has written in restaurants and coffee shops; she has written in hotels, motels, airports, and airplanes; she is writing this paragraph in the research room of a library a mile from her home. She has written outside, inside, late at night, and early in the morning. She has written on a porch; she has written at the beach; she has written at a friend's house; she has written in front of strangers. One time when her computer crashed, she rented computer time at Kinko's and finished her book in the store with its customers and staff conducting their business around her. She has written on typewriters, on computers, and in longhand on legal pads. She has written on napkins and matchbooks, on the backs of her checkbooks and in the margins of magazines. She has written in dribs and drabs, stray sentences here and there, and she has written in marathon sessions lasting way past the time when her body screamed that it wanted to go to bed. She says she would no longer know the "perfect" time and place to write if it came up and bit her.

"The perfect time and place to write is when I'm writing," she says. "Not that some times and places

We take with us rations deemed sufficient to last ten months; for we expect, when winter comes on and the river is filled with ice, to lie over at some point until spring arrives.

—John Wesley Powell

aren't difficult and some arrangements don't drive me mad. They do, but then I just try to write anyway, because I know from long experience that if I can simply get started, I will soon become so preoccupied that nothing in the world will bother me. Just now, for instance, a group of middle-school boys tromped into this library with their teacher. They weren't quiet. He wasn't quiet. Even the librarian was loud. I noticed when they all arrived and sat down, but I didn't hear or see them again until I became vaguely aware that they were leaving."

Preoccupation is the great reward for showing *resolve*.

Resolve is the product of being loyal to your writing.

So if the "perfect" arrangement isn't possible, you do what you have to do to keep writing. That's the nature of resolve. It looks like different things for different writers, which is true of being "preoccupied," too. Lynn says that when she is totally immersed in writing, "Even when I'm doing other things, I'm constantly thinking about the book I want to be working on. When I do sit down to work and I hear, 'You've got mail,' do I wait to finish the sentence I'm writing? Not on your life. I flip to AOL and check my E-mail, my stocks, and pay a few bills while I'm there. Then I go back to writing, until I remember I must change loads in the washer and dryer. I get up and do that. While I'm downstairs, I fix lunch, pet the dogs, rearrange the knickknacks on the coffee table, and then head back upstairs to write."

There's no one way to show resolve. There's no one way to write. But there's only one way to *prove* your resolve, and that's to show the evidence of what you've *written*.

But how does anybody get that kind of resolve?

You get it by thoroughly doing the steps that preceded this one. Each step, fully and honestly done, fuels

We start early this morning, and run along at a good rate until about nine o'clock, when we are brought up on a gravelly bar.

—John Wesley Powell

you for the next one, until by the time you get to this step, you are loaded with energy and resolution. You get it by feeling how miserable you are when you don't get to write; by letting your desire build and build until it's irresistible; by collecting what you need in order to figure out what you want to do and then focusing on that; by saying the words of commitment, "I'm going to write"; by facing your worst fears and comparing them to your dearest desires and making your choice; and by letting go into your writing.

By the way, it's *your* resolve, *your* volition we're talking about now, not anybody else's. You know how you can lead a horse to water but you can't make him drink? Well, somebody else can lead you to your computer, but he can't make you sit there, can he? You're the only one who can decide to do that.

So, as they might have said in Shakespeare's day, "What will you?"

Will you *resolve* to write? That means doing it. That means keeping on doing it. That means finishing it. That means coming back and coming back and coming back to the work. It's just like the resolve Lynn sees in her clients every day in her therapy practice. Her clients come to deal with life issues, step by step, working through their confusion and pain, slogging through the days when nothing seems to be happening. Why do they show such courage and resolve? Because they want to get better, because they want their lives to be better, and by showing up each time, they prove their loyalty to those goals and to their own lives. Because they do that, one day they get better and then their lives get better, and then they accomplish the goals they came with in the beginning, or even more than that.

The late novelist Irwin Shaw once said, "An absolutely

necessary part of a writer's equipment, almost as necessary as talent, is the ability to stand up under punishment, both the punishment the world hands out and the punishment he inflicts upon himself. . . . Failure is more consistent—for everybody—than success."

This is the step you can't fake.

Not quite there yet? Don't worry. Life is generous in its gifts of opportunities to build the muscles of resolve.

Practicing Resolve

If you'd like to deepen your loyalty and resolve, we recommend that you get hold of a book called *The Writer's Journey: Mythic Structure for Writers*, by Christopher Vogler, and look up "Guardians of the Threshold." Remember them? They made their first appearance in the fourth step, Wavering, only we called them trolls. According to Vogler, whose ideas are based on the work of Joseph Campbell and Carl Jung, a guardian of the threshold is anything—any event, person, emotion, *anything*—that stands as a barrier in your path and that will not let you pass unless you prove your worthiness to continue. It could be an illness (your own or somebody else's); it could be the guilt trip you lay on yourself; it could be an unsupportive family member or a critical teacher or reviewer or a rejection letter or even something so mundane as a computer breakdown. It's anything that brings you to a screeching halt and then makes you prove your mettle before continuing.

We've all heard the stories of famous writers whose best-selling books were turned down many, many times before they were finally published. Each of those rejections was a guardian of the threshold for that writer. You just read the story of Nina Osier and the first draft

Today we have an exciting ride. The river rolls down the canyon at a wonderful rate, and, with no rocks in the way, we make almost railroad speed.

—John Wesley Powell

she threw away and her surgery. Those were guardians of the threshold for Nina.

If you can't find the want and willpower to defeat, trick, or somehow get through, by, or around your guardians of the threshold, you will not be able to continue to the end of your writing project. In a metaphorical sense that will feel very real, you will not be "allowed" to go on. It will feel as if there were a secret password, and you don't know what it is. You will be stopped at the gate, even if you can see your goal just there beyond, waiting for you. Without the password, you won't get there. When this happens, your resolve will end in the face of your own personal guardian of the threshold. But if you can get by—ah, then you will continue on with even greater strength and resolve than you had before.

In the course of a writing career, and in the course of any single writing project, you will encounter any number of guardians of the threshold. The trick is to become conscious enough to recognize them when they crop up and then to gird your loins to get by them.

Like Eric Burton did. You want resolve? We'll show you resolve.

Burton, author of *$oft Money*, told us that he wanted to write for most of his life. He said, "I believe that for a writer, there is no decision, there is no realizing that writing would be part of your life; it is always there. You just have to let it out, free that desire that is gnawing away at you." With that attitude, Burton dealt with his guardians of the threshold in a big way. He said, "Sacrifice is the name of the game for the vast majority of writers. If you do not understand that simple fact in the beginning of the process, you are in for a rude awakening. One of the motivating factors for me is the fact that

Start by doing what's necessary, then what's possible and suddenly you are doing the impossible.

—St. Francis of Assisi

I am going blind. I suffer from a degenerative eye disease, and I have learned that despite a handicap, I can do whatever I desire to do. My eyes can only handle a certain amount of time in front of the old computer. I have so much in my head that is just burning to get out. I tend to type slower than the ideas that are swirling around trying to escape their confines. My worst roadblock is time, not the handicap. I wish I had more of it." But you'll note, even that doesn't stop him.

Burton defeats the trolls with his positive outlook. His message to writers is to remember that everyone in this world has something to offer. "Life is a story, and every life has a story to tell," Burton says. "Tell your stories with honor and integrity."

Free to Be Incompetent

While you're busy telling your story with honor and integrity, we are sure you'll meet a troll that all writers meet along the way—incompetence.

Writing (and getting published) is a strange combination of ego and humility. On the one hand, you've got to have enough ego to believe that other people might actually want to read something you write, but on the other hand, you've got to have enough humility to keep at it when the going gets tough. Some of the most practical wisdom we've ever heard is nothing more than—but no less than—a reminder to maintain that important balance between ego and humility while you're working.

If you're getting the impression that writers learn as they go, you're absolutely right. Nobody's perfect even the last time out, much less the first. And that's why it's so important for you to understand that the only way

This day is spent in carrying our rations down to the bay—no small task to climb over the rocks with sacks of flour or bacon. We carry them by stages of about 500 yards each, and when night comes, and the last sack is on the beach, we are tired, bruised, and glad to sleep.

—John Wesley Powell

you'll ever make it clear through this step to Fulfillment is if you're willing to look foolish, make dumb mistakes, start over, revise, change your mind, admit it when you don't know squat, and be as incompetent as you need to be, for as long as you have to be. In our perverse way, we praise incompetence as highly as we praise unhappiness.

Keep writing . . . by staying appropriately humble.

"Appropriately" means not so humble that you think you're slime—slime doesn't have an opposable thumb and can't type, so that attitude is not useful—and not so full of yourself that you think you're the best thing since the alphabet. Appropriate humility is somewhere in be-tween egomaniacal and pond scum. When you hear evil little inner whispers that sound like, "*You* think you can write? This isn't writing, this is dreck," know that's not your humility speaking. That's your ego arrogantly claim-ing that you aren't allowed to write rough first drafts or make the halting efforts of a beginner or write anything less than a classic or perfection. You're not allowed to get stuck for an idea and throw that one away and try again, or go down a wrong-way street with your story and then work to get it going the right way again, or start out by writing shallow characters that might eventually deepen, or get back up on the page and try again after a belly flopper of a rejection.

No, everybody else can make mistakes and learn slowly and fail more often than they succeed and write first drafts that are as feeble as first drafts always are, but you—you're supposed to write a whole draft straight through without running into any problems; and you're supposed to craft perfect sentences every time; and you're supposed to spring full-formed characters out of your soul without having to do the work of getting to

I find I can go no farther, and cannot step back, for I dare not let go with hand, and cannot reach foothold below without. I call to Bradley for help. He finds a way by which he can get to the top of the rock over my head, but cannot reach me. Then he looks around for some stick or limb of a tree, but finds none. Then he suggests that he had better help me with the barometer case; but I fear I cannot hold on to it. The moment is critical. Standing on my toes, my

know them first; and you're not allowed to struggle or work hard or get exhausted by writing (because it's supposed to be smooth and easy and *fun* for you, just you) or have days when the words won't come; and of course, you're supposed to sell everything you write to the first place you send it. If you listen to those hallucinations, you'll never finish anything, and you might not even start.

The good news about true humility—as opposed to the horse's ass of false humility—is that if you can stand being incompetent, you can do anything. There's hardly a published writer living who doesn't feel incompetent at one time or another. Some highly successful ones feel incompetent at least once a day, but they keep going anyway because they *can* stand incompetence. That attitude of practical humility allows them to keep on plugging away, day after day, book after book, royalty check after royalty check.

Talk to a novelist when he's trudging through the middle of his first draft and he'll try to convince you that he can't write, doesn't know what he's doing, never did and never will. The only thing that saves him is that he dimly remembers having felt that way in the middle of all of his previous twenty books, and he got past it. That gives him hope that maybe he can do it again. That, plus the E-mail he gets from his writer friends all saying, "Oh, come on, you always feel this way."

The great thing about incompetence is that there's a cure for it, which is to keep writing and learning until your feelings of competency increase, whether that's in terms of a whole career or any single work. It may surprise you to learn that a lot of mystery and suspense writers feel incompetent writing about police procedure. Many of them never really feel totally secure about their ability to tell it as it is, but they work on curing those feelings of incompetence by doing lots of library and Internet research, by attending classes on criminology, or by interviewing cops. And then they still worry that they've done it incompetently, but they go ahead and write about it as well as they can at the moment—which they may still think isn't good enough—and then their editor loves it, and it gets published anyway to nice reviews, in spite of the single letter they get from a re-tired cop who says they never did it that way where *he* came from.

It's hard to imagine a writer who feels totally compe-tent about every aspect of her work. (There are a few of those, but they go by other names behind their backs. The phrase *horse's ass* comes to mind again.) The truth is, no writer's perfect and no piece of writing is perfect, be-cause perfection is only an idea, and a highly subjective one at that. For every poem you may think is perfection, we could dredge up ten critics who think it's incompe-tent. We've all got areas of *a lack of* expertise—or other people think we do—for which the only cures are hu-mility plus an attitude of dedication to trying to learn how to do it better.

You want to know what "perfect" is?

It's a feeling, not a fact. At least, on this planet, it is. It's the feeling you may sometimes have of a sweet balance between happy confidence and appropriate humility. Of course, new writers feel the most incompetent, but expe-rienced ones can feel incompetent, too. After all, every day is a new one full of things we've never written before. Every page starts out blank. Most writers don't know ex-actly what they're going to write before the words appear in front of their—sometimes surprised—eyes. Writers are always trying new things and feeling quite incompetent

muscles begin to tremble. It is sixty or eighty feet to the foot of the precipice. If I lose my hold I shall fall to the bottom, and then perhaps roll over the bench, and tumble still further down the cliff. At this instant it occurs to Bradley to take off his drawers, which he does, and swings them down to me. I hug close to the rock, let go with my hand, seize the dangling legs, and, with his assistance, I am enabled to gain the top.

—John Wesley Powell

at them. Nonfiction writers who long to write fiction feel like beginners all over again. Poets who have only written with rhyme and meter feel as incompetent as the first fish to come ashore when they attempt free verse. But that fish—or its descendants—eventually developed legs, and so will the poet's later poems. Even the most experienced writers feel incompetent when they try something new, and of course, the truth is that they *are* incompetent at it—until they study and practice it enough to learn how to do it well.

Can you stand to feel incompetent?

If you can increase your ability to stand it, it'll be one of the best gifts you ever give yourself as a writer and person. That increased tolerance for your own incompetence will allow you to try more new things and to persevere at times when otherwise you'd be tempted to give up.

To quote Lawrence Block again, "If you're blocked, lower your sights." That's such a useful philosophy. So is the idea of slowing down, calming down, and breaking down your writing into one small piece at a time, just as an artist carves the feathers on a model duck, single feather by single feather, some of them perfect, some of them not, but all contributing to a whole sculpture. Anne Lamott emphasizes lowering your sights in her popular book about the proper humility of the writer, *Bird by Bird*, meaning take it one scene, one page, one paragraph, one sentence at a time if you have to. That's how whole articles, poems, journals, and books get written.

Dream big but think small.
—Sue Grafton

In keeping with Lynn and Nancy's tendency to live this book as they wrote it, there came a day about midway through the manuscript when Nancy looked at everything she had contributed and hated it. Not only that, but when she read through the current drafts of the chapters, all the words fuzzed in front of her eyes. Nothing made sense to her anymore; she couldn't make heads or tails of it, so how in the hell would a reader? She took a weekend off—having the excuse of an ice storm that knocked out power—but when Monday came around and she knew she'd better get back to work, she felt depressed and confused and didn't know where to start again or what to write.

Taking the advice of other writers—"It's only a book" . . . "Lower your sights" . . . "If you can stand incompetence, you can do anything" . . . "Bird by bird"— she realized the cure was to think of one single thing about the steps that still interested her at that discouraged moment and just start writing about it one sentence at a time. Two hours and five pages later, she had written what you have just read, and while she wasn't entirely back in line with the whole book, she knew she had done a good-enough two hours' work.

Just remember, nobody's perfect, but anybody can be incompetent, even you. Incompetence, what a great place to start! Go ahead and start writing today—we insist on it—even if you suspect that you're probably going to be totally incompetent. If you are, you'll be in great company. We're all out here busily being incompetent, all of us pros and published writers. And besides, you'll get over it. And then you'll try something new and get to be incompetent all over again. It's only natural; it's only the necessary balance between the ego of wanting to be read and the humility of having to do the work of writing first.

If you don't believe us, ask another writer.

In fact, talking to another writer is a very healthy thing to do whenever you're having a hard time staying true to your work.

Perseverance is not a long race; it's many short races one after another.

—Walter Elliott

Separated at Birth?

Writing, as the old saw goes, is a lonely job. It may not seem lonely when you're lost in a fictional world with a plot that seems more real to you than the events recorded in your morning newspaper. And we hope you don't very often feel lonely if you work with a writing partner. And most writers have experienced the blissful solitude that is an escape from a crowded life. But try writing on a full-time professional basis, mostly alone in your office for twenty years, and then you'll probably agree that writing is a lonely job. Solitude, like any good thing, can get to be too much, even for the most introverted of scribblers.

There can be problems with too much alone time. Melancholy, anxiety, antisocial habits, addictions, boredom are a few that come immediately to mind, and what longtime writer hasn't tasted some of those? But another problem seldom discussed is that when you're all alone, you have only your own opinion to trust, and frankly, sometimes it leaves a little something to be desired. You want to be able to take your own word for things, but your own opinions haven't always proved sound. Sometimes, they've lured you down a fruitless path or thrust you into a dead end where there's hardly room to turn around. Sometimes, they've proved so wrong, they've shaken your confidence in yourself and your own best judgment.

As writers, we're usually the only sounding board we have; we must hold all of our best brainstorming sessions with ourselves. It's different for T. J. MacGregor and her husband, Rob MacGregor, who are both full-time professional writers of fiction and nonfiction. They're always bouncing ideas off each other. They read and critique each other's books. They've written books together. But even they, like any good writing pair, eventually wind up staring in solitude at their separate computer screens. Even they must make the vast majority of their writing decisions on their own. The rest of us who aren't married to our best writing friend may toss ideas out to some trusted acquaintances and see what gets tossed back at us, but for the most part, we're making all of our writing decisions on our own, too.

Maybe that's why we treasure our writer friends.

There's a special bond that writers feel with one another that we don't feel with anybody else on earth. This is something of a secret among us, isn't it? It's not something we can easily confide to our husbands or wives or to the best friend we've had since sixth grade. We don't like to tell them, "You know I love you, but sometimes, I just want to be with other writers, because they're the only ones who really understand." We don't want to hurt our loved ones' feelings, but the truth is, *they just don't get it.* Nobody really *gets it* except for other writers and you.

But what is it they don't get?

Oh, Lord, how long is our list? They don't get . . . the overwhelming need and desire to write . . . the drive for solitude in which to work . . . the deep satisfaction of finding the right word, creating dialogue that makes us laugh or cry at our own cleverness, a good hour's writing, finishing a piece . . . the frustration of interruptions . . . how tired we can get from only a couple of hours of writing . . . how insecure we feel sometimes . . . how hard it is to balance the world of diapers and grocery stores with the imaginary world in our heads . . . the dejection of rejection . . . the incredible, universe-altering joy of our first acceptance . . .

Opportunity is missed by most people because it is dressed in overalls and looks like work.

—Thomas A. Edison

It just goes on and on. Have you ever tried to help a nonwriter understand the publishing business? You can't do it; she can't grasp it. It's like no other business and hardly like a business at all in many ways. Have you ever felt the difference between telling a writer friend about an acceptance or a rejection and telling a nonwriter friend? One of them truly gets it and shares it with you, while the other one wants to, and really tries, but just can't do it.

What's more, there are divisions and subdivisions even among writers. Freelancers understand other freelancers, beginners sympathize with other beginners, pros want to hang out with other pros, only another novelist can really understand what it means to write something so long and complex, magazine writers understand one another, nonfiction writers and fiction writers talk over a space they can't quite bridge, poets feel a sense of belonging with other poets, and so on. Which isn't to say that everybody likes everybody else, just that among novelists, for instance, even one you loathe understands what you're going through at the level of personal experience that only another novelist can possibly know.

We need one another in step one, when we're unhappy. Other writers will listen to our moans long after everybody else is sick of us.

We need one another in step two, when we want to be around other people who want the same things we do. There's hardly anything so comforting as a communion of longing, like a lunch group of "prepublished" writers, all aching for that first letter of acceptance.

We need one another in step three, when other writers will understand what it is to decide to commit to this path, to an idea, to an agent, to a contract. They're the ones who can ask you the right questions, based on their own knowledge, which they will share with you.

We need one another in step four, when we're besieged by self-doubt and we need somebody who understands our doubts to listen to us and argue with us or reassure us.

We need one another in step five, when the doubts clear up and we know for sure if it's go or no-go. Only another writer can fully appreciate your courage and daring when you step off into space.

We need one another in step six . . . oh, boy, do we ever need one another in step six. When you're immersed in your work, you can go to your writers lunch and tell them you're a zombie today, and they'll laugh and understand perfectly that your whole head feels drained from all you've emptied out of it. They won't make you talk. You can sit there in a fog, just happy to be around them. When you get blocked or discouraged, you can tell them about it and they'll have wisdom and encouragement to share, and it'll actually mean something to you, because you know *they get it*. They'll be there for you when you need technical writing advice or computer savvy or *anything*, including their printer when yours breaks down on the day you have to get your article/book/story in the mail. They'll be there for you to bitch about your agent, your editor, reviewers, your publicist, and everybody else who sometimes makes your writing life harder instead of easier, and they won't tell you to be nice, and they'll tell you all of their horror stories, too. The adage "Misery loves company" must have been invented to describe writers. They'll read and critique your manuscripts and brainstorm with you, and you will be able to take their advice seriously, because *they get it*.

I've always suspected that if somebody would wire up our heads while we're working, then those times of flow would show up as a blitz of alpha waves.

—Gillian Roberts (Judith Greber)

We need one another in step seven to share and celebrate our accomplishments. Your husband can buy you champagne, your wife can hold a party in your honor, your friends can call and congratulate you, but only another writer will understand to the depths of his soul how very glad you are at this moment.

Of course, not every writer is supportive of other ones; not every writer is a prince of a fellow or a queen among women. Writers don't always get along any more than people in any other field always get along. There can be jealousy, hurt feelings, boredom, aggravation, and all of those other problems that interfere with any relationships. But when it works, when writers are clicking together, it's a more close-knit feeling than we have with any other people on earth.

Those of us who are lucky enough to be published can remember what it felt like to attend a writers conference, to sit among the hundreds of "wanna-bes" in the audience and look up at the successful writers on the stage. It felt good just to be in a group of writers, but we wanted to be in *that* group, we wanted to belong up *there*. Before we ever wrote very much, we wanted just to be included in that special, apparently blessed group of humans who called themselves "writers."

There's a reason why it sometimes seems as if everybody wants to be a writer. Sometimes, it doesn't even have very much to do with writing or with the myth of the get-rich-quick writer or with the supposed glamour of it all. It's even more intangible than that—it's a longing to be able to join this very special community and to feel the bond that writers share only with one another.

So when you're feeling incompetent, search out some writing friends. Believe us, on any given day, they feel every bit as incompetent as you do.

I get very cranky when interrupted. I snap at people, sigh dramatically and slam my door shut.
—Margaret Maron

Choosing Your Depth
of Immersion

Back at the beginning of step four, we watched writer Michael Bane waver in his commitment to go cave diving in the caverns of central Florida. Michael eventually immersed and lived to write about it. Now here's a story of a writer who also came to a big body of water on her writer's path, but her story reached a different conclusion:

The country of Belize sits on the Caribbean on the east coast of Latin America. East of Belize is a big blue hole in the water. It's called, appropriately if unoriginally, the Blue Hole. It's almost perfectly round—one thousand feet in diameter and more than four hundred feet deep. It's a spooky sight from the air or the water, because it looks so incongruously and ominously dark blue as compared to the pretty, perfect azure of the shallows around it. The Blue Hole, a holy grail of scuba divers, is estimated to be between ten thousand and fifteen thousand years old. It was once a sinkhole whose roof caved in during an ice age. Most of the things to "see" inside of the Blue Hole cling to its walls as if they're afraid of falling in; dolphins, sharks, and barracudas prowl around it, but there aren't many sea creatures to be found within its depths.

Those empty depths frighten some people more than others.

A few years ago, Nancy accompanied a boatload of scuba-diving tourists out to the Blue Hole. She does not scuba. She is, in fact, seriously afraid of swimming in oceans, preferring merely to sit beside them and admire them. But on this day, she had decided to try snorkeling, though the few times she had attempted it before, she

I've always felt that writing should be an act of discovery, but when it truly became that, I was taken by surprise. I was writing my first novel and something bad happened to one of the characters. Not only did I not expect it to happen, I didn't want it to happen. The entire time I was tapping out that scene, I was putting on brakes, trying to stop the action. When I finished, I put my hands to my face. My cheeks were wet. I had no idea I'd been crying while I was writing.

—Judy Goldman

hadn't enjoyed it very much. She had never mastered the simple equipment. Water went up her nose. Salt got in her eyes. She tended to kick the flippers against her own legs instead of against the water. And at least once when she'd tried it, some of her swimming partners had been sharks.

But on the theory that everything in a writer's life is research, and on the equally foolhardy theory that everything that requires courage makes you a better writer, "I paid my money and got on the damned boat."

It rocked, and she felt seasick.

First, they stopped near a reef so the divers could warm up with a practice dive. While they explored the deeper layers, Nancy paddled around in her face mask and flippers, trying to have fun but feeling as tense as a line pulled taut.

After that brief foray, the tour operators served sandwiches on the boat.

"The scuba divers ate heartily. My stomach declined the gift."

And then came the big moment—their arrival near the Blue Hole. The pilot of the boat put down the anchor. The scuba divers plunged in. Much more slowly and tentatively, Nancy awkwardly lowered herself into the water with her snorkeling gear.

The water was rough; waves splashed her mask and rolled her around.

"I looked up at the boat, and one of the crew pointed me toward the Blue Hole. With my heart pounding against my swimming suit, I began to paddle in that direction. The closer I got, the rougher the water seemed to get, so that I felt as if I were fighting the ocean and it was fighting me. Was it trying to give me a message? *You don't belong here! Go back, go back!*"

Then she saw the water change color, because of the change of depth.

"It was uncanny how dramatically it changed from aqua to navy blue."

Adrenaline flooded her body, screaming *Flight*!

"I was literally afraid of dying. I told myself I was being silly. So what if the bottom dropped out? I'd still be swimming on the top. Nothing was going to happen to me. Swimmers and divers went in there all the time, and nothing happened to them. I forced myself to continue to the edge, and then I made myself swim over it."

Panic. She felt nothing but panic.

"I hurried back to the rim. I couldn't get back to it fast enough. Then I just kept paddling madly, fighting back through the waves to get to the boat. I was exhausting myself; I could hardly take a breath. You'd have thought a great white shark was after me. That's how scared I was. I scrambled back on that boat faster than most of the scuba divers had jumped off of it, and I huddled there until they returned. That night, back at my hotel, I shivered with chills, sweated with a fever, and threw up for hours."

She came, she saw, she did not conquer—and lived to write about it anyway.

Not everybody immerses all of the way every time. Sometimes when we waver, our fears and doubts are too big for us this time, and we back off. We just can't let go. And so we never reach this step of Immersion. And sometimes, that's the right decision for us at the time. We do the best we can. We dive as deep into the ocean, into our lives, into our relationships, and into our writing as we are capable of doing at any given time. And live to write about *that*, too.

It's *all* material, even when we only go partway into it.

It's a help for writing in that I tend to live in my fantasy world for days at a time without interruption. It's bad in that I tend to lose track of the things going on around me including missing important events in my friends' lives.

—Jeffrey Marks

The secret is to immerse as far as you can, as well as you can, even if that's not anywhere near all the way, and even if your abilities aren't very great right now. Next time, you will know more, and you may feel more confident. Next time, Nancy may swim out farther. Maybe someday, she'll take scuba-diving lessons. And maybe the Blue Hole will freeze over. And next time, any one of us may dive deeper into our writing than we ever have before—if we want to, and if we understand that this is the nature of step six on the writer's path.

Immersion. It can look like snorkeling, or it can look like diving into a Blue Hole; it can go shallow or deep—but when you do it with all of your attention and with resolve, it's genuinely immersion, no matter how other people may measure it. *You're* the measure of your own immersion; only you will know if you went as far as you can go; only you will know the joy of doing it; and only you will know the disappointment of failing to go as deep and as far as you can at the time.

We know a young basketball player who was always considered to be an athlete of great promise. Although he developed into a high-school star, he never achieved what he and everybody else always knew he could. This happened even though he dearly loved the game and even though he never felt forced by anybody to play it competitively.

"I never really tried to take it as far as I might have," he'll tell you. "I always meant to, but somehow, I just never did it. I didn't do the running I could have done to stay in shape; I didn't lift the weights. I'm good, but I'll always wonder what might have been."

Is that something he'll regret all his life?

"Probably," he says.

He's only twenty years old, but that chance is over for him.

A writer is more lucky. Our chances are never over. Never.

The reward for Immersion is so great. It's not only the joy of achieving the furthest limits of your own potential, it's also the only route through to the last step on the writer's path, Fulfillment.

Take your work seriously but yourself lightly.
—C. W. Metcalf

Fulfillment

Step Seven on the Writer's Path

· ·

I feel successful when the writing goes well. This lasts five minutes. Once, when I was on the best-seller list, I also felt successful. That lasted three minutes.

—Jacqueline Briskin

Many of life's failures are people who did not realize how close they were to success when they gave up.

—Thomas Edison

Dear Herr Doctor: You are already 10 months behind with the manuscript of Das Kapital, *which you have agreed to write for us. If we do not receive the manuscript within 6 months, we shall be obliged to commission another to do this work.*

—Letter to Karl Marx from his Leipzig publisher

So when Karl Marx sat down to write *Das Kapital*, was he thinking, "Do I need an agent? What about subrights? Can I get a movie deal?" And yet, when we speak with emerging writers, the questions they ask are all about step seven—Fulfillment—and what they usually mean by that is getting published or produced. No wonder they get discouraged along the path: they are trying to start at the end instead of at the beginning.

Which isn't to say that getting published isn't also fulfilling. As novelist Vinnie Hansen says, "Published. It's a magic word for aspiring writers. When I published *Murder, Honey,* my first novel, I was no more of a writer than I had been in the past, but the tangible product made me a writer in others' eyes. I loved this shift in my identity, the increased stature."

The poet Marge Piercy has wryly observed that we're not given much credit for having talent until *after* we're published. Before that, she says in a poem called "For the Young Who Want To," "what you have is a tedious delusion, a hobby like knitting."

The trick, we believe, is to love the knitting and to get that done first.

And so this step is partly about putting things in their proper order and partly about enjoying and celebrating them when you do. If you never quite manage to get to fulfillment, or if you don't get here as often as you'd like, let's look at why that might be.

I Don't Get No Satisfaction!

This problem of wanting the reward before we do the work—we might call it premature emancipation—afflicts even longtime professional writers.

"Sometimes, when I'm working on a book," Nancy confesses, "I'll get blocked because I start worrying about how big or important it should be in order to attract a lot of attention and sell a lot of books."

When that happens, she has put her publishing cart before her writing horse.

Sure, you can motivate yourself with the dream of being published, but if you let it take over, you're likely to stall out before it ever comes true. "But what about James Patterson?" we can hear you say, of the best-selling

By perseverance the snail reached the arc.

—Charles Haddon Spurgeon

writer. "He says he purposely set out to write a best-seller. So did John Grisham and a lot of other famous writers." True, quite a few very successful writers have approached the field with studied purposefulness, but you might want to make note of the fact that they still had to write the books that got them there. You can study how to write a best-seller until you could give lectures on how to do it, but knowledge alone won't land you on anybody's best-seller list. Only actual writing will do that for you. And that requires keeping that ol' cart behind that ol' horse, no matter who you are or what kind of cart you're driving. Tiger Woods could have memorized the layout of every golf course in the world, but if he hadn't practiced for thousands of hours, all he'd be by now is a young golf fan with a very good memory. The Williams sisters, Serena and Venus, could have plotted their rise to the top of the tennis world for years, but if they hadn't spent those same years whacking a million tennis balls, they'd only be girls with a plan but no trophies. They had their "horse" of practice and hard work back up there in front of their "cart" of ambition, right where it should be.

You don't want to be like the beginning writer who said to us, "I'm not concerned about how good my manuscript is when I send it in, because I know that an editor will whip it into shape for me." When we heard that, we knew she was doomed. She will wait a long, long time before that ever happens.

So we have to ask you: where's your cart, and where's your horse?

Here are some other telltale things that writers say that alert us to improper horse/cart placement. You'll have to pardon us if our answers sound a bit jaded; we've heard these more times than you'd care to know:

My first thought was to cheer and celebrate the fact that my obituary wouldn't read, "She wrote a book once." Then I went out and ran around the house squealing in glee. My house is isolated. This wouldn't disturb the neighbors. Then I went back to my computer as though I'd had an injection of adrenaline.

—Carmen Clark

"Should I copyright it first?" (You should write it first.) "What if I send a query to several publishers and they all want it?" (You should only have such problems. Just worry about writing it.) "What if somebody steals my ideas?" (Just write the damned thing. If you're worried about burglars, get a gun.) "I've written three chapters of a novel. Should I start sending it out to agents now?" (No, you should write Chapter 4 now.) "I was thinking of sending my poems out now and waiting to do any rewriting until I hear what the editors have to say." (We're thinking you should rewrite them now, or you will never hear from any editors.)

Etcetera.

Sometimes you earn more doing the jobs that pay nothing.

—Todd Ruthman

Whatever your question, our answer is: write. And then, rewrite. We know you wouldn't have got this far if you didn't know that and do that. But sometimes, we all need to be reminded that the road to fulfillment is to put the writing first, last, and always.

We're grown-ups here—we can manage to hold two thoughts in our minds at the same time: (1) that we have big ambitions for our writing and (2) that we are humble and practical enough to write one syllable at a time.

If you can manage to do that, you'll never sound like the beauty contestants whom Jay Leno was mocking when he joked, "As Miss America, my goal is to bring peace to the world and then get my own apartment."

Dare to Dream Small

It's OK to dream big—more than OK, or there wouldn't be a second step called Wanting—but don't forget to dream small, too. While you're visualizing that Nobel Prize in literature, also visualize yourself at the keyboard today. And tomorrow and the day after that.

When you fantasize about getting that acceptance letter from *The New Yorker*, also picture yourself rewriting, learning, growing, and working hard. Go ahead and post that affirmation "I am a *New York Times* best-selling author," but while you're at it, post another one, too: "I wrote today." The outcome of our big dreams of fulfillment may not turn out to be what we think they will be, but we can always make our small dreams of fulfillment come true, just by putting a word down on paper. Too often, we tend to visualize the pot of gold at the end of the rainbow and forget the long, hard trek to get there. The trek itself is fulfilling.

On the other hand, when it comes to writing, sometimes it's just as well that we don't know everything ahead of time. In fact, it's probably a damned good thing that most of us don't really know what we're getting into before we start. Gene Fowler expressed this idea with a bit of exaggeration when he said, "Writing is easy. All you do is stare at a blank sheet of paper until drops of blood form on your forehead."

Don't kid yourself. The writing life can be a lot like a pregnancy and delivery and the subsequent raising of children. If parents knew what was in store for them before they started, it could possibly be the end of civilization. How many women would get pregnant knowing the pain of labor? How many parents would have children if they knew how much pain can accompany the joys of raising a family? And how many writers would start a novel, for instance, if they really knew anything about the publishing world?

But all suffering has an ending, even if it's death. Hey, we're trying to be cheerful here, which isn't easy when you're talking about publishing. As with labor, at some

The reward for work well done is the opportunity to do more.

—Jonas Salk

point down the line, unless you're really stuck somewhere earlier on the path, your suffering will end, and your writing will be born.

How Do You Spell Fulfillment?

You would think that seeing your "baby" born would be the moment of fulfillment for any writer, wouldn't you? For some writers, it certainly is. Kris Neri says that when she received two copies of her first book, *Revenge of the Gypsy Queen,* "My hands just shook as I opened the package. Since I tend to be emotional, I thought I would cry, but I didn't. Well, maybe just a little. But mostly, my face was stretched as wide as it would go with the biggest grin I'd ever produced. I carried the book to my living room and placed it on the coffee table, where I just stared at it for the longest time, before finally holding it in my arms."

For others, like Nora Roberts, fulfillment comes even earlier—when their work first receives some kind of outside validation. "A moment when a writing dream came true for me was my first sale," Nora told us. "I honestly don't think anything can top it. I remember mine came in midsummer of 1980. My kids were fighting, as usual. It was murderously hot, and I'd just stepped, barefoot, on a hugely fat tick one of the dogs had scratched off onto the kitchen floor. When the phone rang, the last thing I expected was a voice from New York telling me Silhouette was buying my book. I paced back and forth, leaving bloody footprints on the kitchen floor, trying to take it in while my kids murdered each other. It was one of the most beautiful moments of my life."

These characters persisted in annoying the writer until she finally set down their story, after which they were kind enough to leave her alone.
—Nina Osier

Then again, the moment can come very late for some writers.

Elmer Williams said that his writing dream came true when he finished a book he had started thirty-four years earlier. Other authors echoed his sentiments about fulfillment's coming after a long career. Sandra Rubin, who's an artist rather than a writer, nevertheless speaks for mature artists of all sorts when she says of her painting, "Working, working . . . like magic this current painting in progress has gradually transformed from a flat surface to something with a life of its own. To be at this stage in my life with my 'gift' is the biggest reward of all."

The elation of fulfillment can also creep up, as expressed by E. L. Doctorow, who said, "As the book goes on, it [the ending] becomes inevitable. . . . You know before you get there what the last scene is. Sometimes what the last line is. But even if none of that happens, even if you find yourself at the end before you expected to, a kind of joy breaks over you, spills out of your eyes. And you realize you've finished."

There's just no way to predict when fulfillment will come.

In fact, finishing a project isn't always even a positive experience. For some authors, it's a big letdown, as poet Marianne Moore expressed: "I feel somewhat at a loss, aimless and foolishly sentimental, and disconnected, when I've finished one work and haven't yet become absorbed in another."

For other writers, such as Lynn, it's not enough to write something if nobody wants to buy it, publish it, or read it. If the book isn't on the shelves at the bookstore and isn't being read and isn't being helpful to people,

Fall seven times, stand up eight.

—Japanese proverb

then Lynn does *not* feel fulfilled. As much as she loves to write, her real enthusiasm isn't for the writing, it's for sales, but not because of the money or the fame. "To me," she says, "sales represent how important my message is, how helpful my information, and whether or not readers are actually finding ways to apply my ideas to their own lives."

"The payoff for me," writer Norm Harris agrees, "is not any money gained from the book sales but rather the joy my written words might bring to others. When I first sat down to write, my goal was to write a story that someday would find its way into the hands and into the imagination of some kid in Tulsa, Oklahoma. Today, I feel that I have been rewarded and that I have accomplished that goal."

We know, you're probably thinking, "That's easy for him to say. He got paid!"

But John Steinbeck also once said, "I truly do not care about a book once it is finished. Any money or fame that results has no connection in my feeling with the book. The book dies a real death for me when I write the last word. I have a little sorrow and then go on to a new book which is alive."

Maybe you're still thinking, "Oh, sure, that's easy for a famous writer to say."

But the truth is that there are many of us who love the process of writing a lot more than we love finishing it. Partly, to be honest, that's because when we come up out of our writer's den, there's a whole world out there that may or may not love what we have done. There are editors and agents who may reject us, readers who may not be interested in our work, and critics who may disparage it. Walking the writer's path has been hard at

Throw in a few tumescent penises and breasts like upright cones and you can put in that new swimming pool or make your annual contribution to The Cat Wilhelmina Guerilla Unit of the Animal Rights Liberation Army.
—Mark Helprin

times, but now we're coming to the place where we have to reveal where we've been and what we've been doing, and that's an intimidating prospect to many of us. It's not like bursting through the tape at the finish line of the New York City Marathon, where you get accolades just for finishing, no matter what. But what if you ran those twenty-six miles, and when you stopped, the people around you turned their backs on you or criticized the way you ran the race or threw Gatorade in your face?

That's what some writers fear about finishing, that there will be no reward for them, no victory lap, no medal on a ribbon, and no prize money and that they will stumble away from all that effort with their hearts broken. Some are so scared of that prospect that they never show their work to anybody, or they never rewrite, or they never take the risk of submitting it for publication. Or they do it once, get badly bitten, and withdraw again. They keep their precious words hoarded close to their hearts or hidden under their beds or stuffed way back in their closets, and so they never even get the chance to feel the deep satisfaction that only comes from bringing their completed work into the world. For an artist, that kind of situation is tragic, like a pregnancy that ends in stillbirth.

It isn't always fear that makes a writer dread the end, however.

There can be positive reasons for it, too. If you're like Lynn, for instance, you may not want something good to come to an end. "The only endings I look forward to," she says, "are the ones that follow doing something I dislike, like cleaning house or paying bills or balancing my checkbook. But when I'm doing something I enjoy, like writing, I'd be happy for it to go on and on."

Remember how some writers said that when the words are really flowing, it's better than sex? *That's* why some of them don't want it to stop. They're like runners who say, "I felt as if I just wanted to keep running forever."

And yet, knowing something will eventually end is part of what gives it that rich flavor while you're doing it. "On second thought, I guess the endings are partly why I enjoy the process," Lynn admits. "If the process had no definition, I'd probably get sick of it at some point. Knowing there is an end is part of the reason I am very much in the moment of what I am doing. And I also notice that as the ending approaches, I start working on the next proposal, so that, to borrow one of Nancy's favorite clichés, I can keep my dance card full."

And yet this step, Fulfillment, is not really about endings per se. It's not necessarily about getting published or even about finishing your final rewrite or typing "The End." Yes, you may be on this step when you type "The End," but it can also come at the end of a good day of writing and at the end of a good sentence. It's only sometimes about finishing an entire writing project; it's also about the feeling of earned reward for *anything* you accomplish on this path. It's the writer's medal on a ribbon, your trophy, your pat on the back for anything along the way that gives you a feeling of fulfillment.

Fulfillment is the step at which you celebrate your milestones—the strides toward accomplishing what you wanted to do today or tomorrow or next year or anywhere along the writer's path. You don't have to have done it perfectly, and don't worry, you probably won't. In order to win the satisfying prize of fulfillment, you "only" have to make an honest, continuing effort, and the best news is that you can keep winning it all of your

I don't want to get to the end of my life and find that I lived just the length of it. I want to have lived the width of it as well.

—Diane Ackerman

life. John Wesley Powell only got to go down the Grand Canyon once, but you can walk the writing path every day of your life if you want to.

For many writers, that's the greatest fulfillment of all.

On a writing trip to Florida, Lynn and Nancy sat on the balcony of their condo watching a fisherman catch one fish after another, pausing only long enough to throw them back into the Atlantic. Here was clearly a person who understood the message: there is no finish line. For him, the time spent fishing was the be-all and end-all—his fulfillment. And he clearly understood the concept of emptying the pitcher to make room for more. Throwing one fish back and rebaiting his hook seemed to make room for an endless string of new fish.

Ending without Fulfillment

Sadly, some people aren't so easily contented. We hear stories all the time of those who get all the way to this last step on their writer's path, only then to experience a complete lack of fulfillment. Some of them are people who can't seem to finish anything. Some are people who do finish, but because they are very hard on themselves, or they are so focused on the next job, they can't ever seem to relax and savor the moment. They remind us of people who quit smoking a dozen times or who gain and lose the same fifty pounds again and again. Over and over, they succeed—they *succeed*—and yet they never feel it. Because they don't feel it, it seeps away. Then, when they start again, the work feels harder than ever, because they never quite believe it or enjoy that respite of joy and celebration.

We've done versions of that a few times ourselves.

"The first time I had a book accepted," Nancy recalls,

I have balance. I write in the morning or evening, a little bit each day. I do better in the morning. Evening has more distractions. I have a place . . . a cabin in the woods on the shore of the ocean a half mile from where Erle Stanley Gardner wrote his mysteries. When I was a kid, we'd go down there,

"I was overwhelmed with joy, and I told myself to be sure to remember every moment of that day. But then, by the time I'd published several books, I had become so blasé, and also so weighed down by responsibilities, that when cartons of my latest book arrived, I shoved them aside with my foot, without even opening the box, and I walked away! I was several feet into my living room before it hit me what I had done. I was horrified at myself. I hurried back to open a carton, took out a book, caressed it, admired it, and tried to recapture some of my original pride and gratitude."

If you have a hard time reaching fulfillment—like a maiden reaching orgasm—we suggest that you go backward through the previous steps, taking them slowly, and reviewing them to make sure you've really dug deep and done them to the best of your ability. We believe that when you do that, you'll burst through to a more delicious finale.

But what if you don't get that far? What if you get scared or distracted, and you stop before fulfillment? That nearly happened to John Wesley Powell after a series of harrowing episodes as his party floated through the Grand Canyon. "I almost conclude to leave the river," he admits, in his diary. "But for years I have been contemplating the trip. To leave the exploration unfinished . . . having already almost accomplished it, is more than I am willing to acknowledge, and I determine to go on."

Have you been contemplating your writing trip for years? If so, we hope you will not leave your own exploration unfinished, not if there are still parts of your creativity to explore, not when you are so close to doing it. Wouldn't that be more than you would be willing to acknowledge? We hope you will determine to go on, so that you can say, as Powell did one day in his diary . . .

the bodyguard was there. . . . I learned Gardner had to recluse himself and make sure there were no distractions. So I said, I've got to do this. So I sit by water, play music, write, and go for hours and the time disappears, smoke cigars, drink my wine. . . . So much fun.

—Norm Harris

I turned off my computer, went downstairs to make lunch and said, "I just finished my first book."

—Gary Legwold

"A very hard day's work has been done."

Those individual hard days of work will accumulate, one by one, until you will understand Powell's emotion when he wrote, "The relief from danger, and the joy of success are great. How beautiful the sky; how bright the sunshine; what 'floods of delirious music' pour from the throats of birds; how sweet the fragrance of earth, and tree, and blossom!" Sounding nearly delirious with happiness himself, he continued, "Now the danger is over; now the toil has ceased; now the gloom has disappeared; now the firmament is bounded only by the horizon; and what a vast expanse of constellations can be seen!"

We know just how he felt.

And then, when you have rested, regenerated, and recovered from this latest journey, after you have celebrated its conclusion and savored the feeling of fulfillment, then you can gather your supplies, stuff them in your backpack one more time, fill your water bottle, put on your walking shoes, and start along the writer's path again. And again. And then, with any luck, again. Sometimes, you'll even find yourself on it again before you know it, as Nancy did.

"On Friday night when I stepped into the shower, I felt so unhappy that it clicked in my mind: 'I'm back in step one again. But how could that be?' I had reached a fulfillment milestone, sending off the first two-thirds of a book to my editor. That was clearly a step seven moment, so how could I be back in step one? Easy. It happens all the time.

"I realized that I had been thrown back into step one the previous Tuesday, when my editor called to tell me what she thought of the first chunk of my book. 'I'm excited about it,' she said, but then she went on to list four suggestions for me. I knew she was right the minute I heard what they were, and I realized that if I could do them, it would result in a much better novel, but I also knew they were going to mean a lot of hard work and rethinking that I didn't want to have to do. I was exhausted from the first 254 pages. The last thing I wanted to hear was, 'Needs more work.'

"I made myself start to labor on it anyway in fits and starts for the next four days, but that didn't mean I was happy about it. By the time I turned on the water in the shower on Friday night, I felt ready to burst from the misery and anxiety of feeling overworked, overwhelmed, underqualified, and as burned out as a candle whose wick is stuck in the wax.

" 'OK, if I'm unhappy, this must be step one,' I said to myself as the water poured down. 'Hello again, step one. I hate you.'

" 'I want out of this,' I thought. I wished the water could wash me clear off this damned step. But that kind of 'wanting' was apparently not enough to propel me out of step one and fully into step two. It had only been enough so far to keep me working just enough to salve my conscience. It had only been enough to keep me at the grindstone because I 'wanted' not to feel the anxiety I would feel if I didn't write at all.

" 'You're supposed to be the expert on these steps,' I muttered. 'So if you're so damned smart, how would you tell yourself to deal with this?'

"The answer that came was the usual one: Do it thoroughly.

"But I already felt totally unhappy, so how could I do it *better*?

"Well, first I concentrated on how it felt in my

> *They can't yank a novelist like they can a pitcher. A novelist has to go the full nine, even if it kills him.*
>
> —Ernest Hemingway

body—the heavy feeling in my chest, the lump at the back of my throat, the tears lurking just behind my eyes. Then I totally surrendered to that honest misery, allowing myself to feel and resent all of it as deeply and unsparingly as I could.

" 'I am so unhappy,' I confessed to myself, and then I wailed self-pityingly inside my head, 'When is this ever going to end?!'

"The answer to that was: 'Oh, in about five minutes.'

"The mysterious alchemy that happens when we let ourselves surrender fully to any given step began to sizzle while I was still in the shower, although I didn't realize it then. Hardly aware I was even doing it, I began to think about the book. An idea occurred to me. When I got out and crawled into bed, I grabbed a notebook and wrote down that scene. And then a new character appeared in my head. I wrote down that scene, too. When I finished, I turned off the light and lay down to sleep. It was nearly midnight by that time. After a short period of lying there feeling restless, I realized I'd never get to sleep at that rate. 'I may as well get up and work,' I thought. By the time I was up and on my feet, I realized with a happy little jolt that the misery was gone from my body and my heart.

"I was now filled with an eager desire to make some coffee and rewrite my new scenes onto the computer. I was on step two—Wanting.

" 'Let's do it,' I thought, which put me on step three—Commitment.

"On my way to the computer, I felt some step four—Wavering—qualms about whether or not it was such a good idea to be making coffee and staying up so late working. And then I surrendered and Let Go—step five—and moments later, I was fully Immersed in working again, step six. Blessed step seven—Fulfillment—arrived at 3:30 A.M. as I printed out all of the new pages for one of the scenes I had earlier written in longhand.

"When I lay in bed again, and just before I fell easily asleep, I had to laugh at myself, because I was already feeling a little unhappy again. 'Here I go, back to step one again,' I thought, but it wasn't so bad this time. Now I was oriented on the path; I knew where I was. And in the morning, I'd have that other whole new scene to rewrite into the computer. It felt like knowing I had the makings of a good breakfast in my tent.

"I had just proved to myself once again that step one doesn't have to last forever if I'm willing to be honest with myself about it. 'Well, I'm here at step one,' is what I had thought resignedly in the shower, 'so I may as well just do it.' "

It is common to go back again and again to step one and then to take all of the following steps to get to a satisfactory stanza, a chapter, a rewrite, a single word. That's normal. That's the process. It's called "writing." Sometimes, it sucks.

It's never too soon to start out on this path, and it's never too late, either. You know the old saying "Fishermen never die. They just smell that way"? Well, if fishermen can do what they love forever, so can we. Besides, it takes even less equipment to write than it does to fish, and we don't even need water. We can continue to write as long as our synapses keep firing and as long as we can lift pen to paper.

Fulfillment without Ending

We meet writers who tell us that they'd love to write but that it's too late for them. They seem to believe they've

After supper, we sit by our campfire, made of driftwood caught by the rocks, and tell stories of wild life; for the men have seen such in the mountains, or on the plains, and on the battlefields of the South.

—John Wesley Powell

passed some point of no return, after which they can't hope to write or to be published. But thinking such sad thoughts doesn't keep their hearts from longing. They still "want," but they think it's too late for them ever to have what they want. And by believing that, they're making it come true.

It is never too late. Mystery writers, for instance, usually don't even get started until middle age, and some a great deal later than that. Barbara Comfort published her first mystery novel when she was eighty; at our last count, she's up to three books now. Virginia Rich started writing novels when she was sixty-three; by the time she died, at seventy-two, she also had three books out. They didn't allow themselves to be stopped by age any more than other writers allow themselves to be hindered by other obstacles. T. S. Eliot was a banker all his life and a poet, too. In fact, most writers hold jobs besides writing, often a full-time job or more than one job. Writers have families to take care of, children to raise, spouses to consider. Everybody has something to work around or overcome. At age seventy-six, Elmer Williams said it best: "I realize I need to cram everything into my remaining years that I can. I have three more books I feel I must write, God willing, and two of those are well on their way."

While we were working on this book, the woman who wrote twenty-four of the first Nancy Drew novels, Mildred Wirt Benson, died at the age of ninety-six. Two days before her death, she wrote an article, a tribute to public libraries, for her weekly newspaper column in the *Toledo Blade*. She was a writer up to the very end, as any of us can be, too.

The Never-Ending Journey

Thank you for coming along with us on the writer's path.

We'll be leaving you here—except we're really not, because you can come back to this book anytime you need to check the map. The truth is, although you'll write alone, you'll never really be alone unless you choose to be, because you're part of a huge fraternity of other writers, all along this path. We have a deep, rich history, you know. Granted, some of your fellow travelers here are ghosts, but there are plenty of us still in flesh and blood, as well. Look for us around the campfire. We'll share our latest stories with you, just as so many writers generously shared theirs for this book, and we look forward to hearing yours. In the meantime, we wish you Godspeed and travel mercies. May you be deeply blessed by unhappiness, wanting, commitment, wavering, letting go, immersion, and fulfillment, and then may you be blessed by them again.

The perfect journey is circular—the joy of departure and the joy of return.
—Dino Basili

Appendix I

Quick Finder: How Can I Tell Which Step I'm On?

● ●

Here is a list of the key words that sum up how to recognize each step, along with some thoughts, feelings, and behaviors that typify each step. Use this as a handy guide to help you find and work the step you are on.

The *key words* for step one, **Unhappiness,** are *feel* and *reveal*.

You may experience this step as a state of feeling dry and restless and of thinking there must be something better in life, of finding praise hollow and your current work meaningless. You may be having *thoughts* like, "I wish I could do something different. I wish I knew what I wanted to do. Maybe I should give up writing. I think I'll die if I have to keep living this way."

You may be *feeling* despondent, unfulfilled, in despair, uninspired, not enthusiastic, bored, stuck, anxious, ashamed, fearful, angry, miserable, hopeless.

Telltale *behaviors* are: wishing, writer's block, procrastination, worrying about when your next project is due but not working on it, looking busy but not being busy with your real work, constantly comparing yourself to others and yet always falling short, trudging.

The *key words* for step two, **Wanting,** are *focus* and *collect*.

You're sick and tired of being sick and tired. You want it, you

want it bad, and you want it now. Your *behaviors* may
be: moping about; pouting; whining and complaining
about how bad you feel, how unfair life is, how unlucky
you are, how everyone else always gets all the good ideas
or the lucky breaks. Other behaviors include more comparing of yourself to others, being demanding, asking,
and begging. Typical *feelings* include longing, jealousy,
insecurity, self-pity, frustration, anger. Typical *thoughts*
include "I never get what I want. Why does it take so
long? How can I wait any longer? Everyone else gets the
breaks. I'm unlucky. Other people have what I want."

The *key words* for step three, **Commitment,** are *decide*
and *set in motion*.

"I'm going to do it" is the phrase that tells you you're
here. Your options begin to focus, you see a possibility,
and you choose it. You *feel* energized, excited, happy, relieved, focused, high, hopeful, eager, anticipatory. You're
thinking, "I'm going to make dates, plans, set deadlines.
I've made my decision, and it feels great. I can't wait to
get started. I'm on my way. I can do it. Yes!" Your *behaviors* may include scheduling, planning, organizing, brainstorming, creating outlines, working on a proposal,
clearing a calendar, getting a few words down on paper.

The *key words* for step four, **Wavering,** are *face fears*
and *align core values*.

Now you're worried again. "I think I can," you say,
"but what if I can't?" Suddenly, you're *feeling* self-doubt,
scared, malaise, anxious, restless, stupid, unsure, discouraged, overwhelmed, panicked, tired. "What if I
can't actually do it?" you may be *thinking*, or, "Where do
I go from here? What will everyone say if I change my
mind? What if my writing is awful? What if I fail? I
must have been crazy to think I could do this/agree to do
this/promise to do this. This project is too big. I'm in

over my head." Suddenly, you *behave* like this: you may find yourself lying on your back staring at the ceiling again or playing too many computer games, searching the Web for "interesting" items, shopping on eBay, shopping anywhere, going to the movies, watching TV, playing cards, sleeping a lot, eating a lot, drinking a lot, going through old outlines and books, taking another class, getting overinvolved in other people's lives and problems, dreaming up worst-case scenarios, depressing or scaring yourself to death.

The *key words* for step five, **Letting Go,** are *release* and *cross over*.

Peace, relief, freedom, exhilaration, joy, and lightness are the welcome *feelings* associated with this step. You also may feel suddenly unencumbered, an adrenaline rush, a bit scared but excited, eager, justified, smug, centered, triumphant. You may be *thinking*, "Amazing. Wow. Whew. Thank goodness. Now I can do it. I'm glad that's over. Can't wait to get started again." Or, "I can't wait to really get down to it this time." If you've let go of an idea and decided not to do it, you also may be thinking, "Well, at least now I know. I'm relieved that's over. I'm relieved I didn't make that mistake. I can get on with the rest of my life now." Your *behaviors* include taking risks, leaping into the unknown, showing courage, taking a leap of faith, and allowing yourself to be vulnerable. Telltale signs are: doors opening for you, help arriving, guidance, happy coincidences and synchronicities, good fortune, a feeling that all's right with the world and everything's working out as it is meant to do.

The *key words* for step six, **Immersion,** are *resolved* and *preoccupied*.

You just want to hide out and write or work on something to do with your writing. There isn't enough time in the day. Every interruption drives you crazy. You're *thinking*, "I want to be alone. I don't want to stop. I wish the phone would quit ringing. I wonder if I'll have any friends left by the time I'm finished? My neck, shoulders, and back hurt. Why is the refrigerator so empty? Where did all my clean clothes go?" You're *feeling* tired, achy, and jazzed. You may feel guilty for ignoring everything and everybody else. When this step is going well, you're focused, in a trance, blissed-out, or oblivious, but when it's going badly, you're frustrated, nervous, worried, annoyed, irritable. Someone looking at you from the outside would immediately recognize these *behaviors* as the telltale signs: you're lost in your work; making yourself inaccessible; surrounded by papers, books, moldy coffee cups; and you probably don't look so hot yourself. But the work is getting done, and that's all that matters to you right now.

The *key words* for step seven, **Fulfillment,** are *celebration*, *endings*, and *beginnings*.

There is a sense of joy and relief, which may be brief because soon you'll start the whole process over again. Sometimes, this step *feels* as exhilarating as crossing a finish line; other times, it feels like a big letdown, like coming off a high. You're *thinking*, "I really did it. What now? Will it make the best-seller list? Will it sell well? Can I go shopping now? Can I do it again? Can I take a break? I'm rad! That wasn't so hard. Wow. I'm going to pat myself on the back for figuring out what to do with that paragraph." However you feel or think, here's what we want to see you *do*: celebrate, or at least stop long enough to notice and appreciate what you've just accomplished, however large or small. If you need to, pause long enough to allow your creative well to fill up again. After a large chunk of writing or a long day, rest and rejuvenate yourself, have some fun, raise a toast, clean up, get back in shape, get reacquainted with your friends and family.

And remember, no matter how good you feel right now, you will eventually start to feel itchy or unhappy again. Expect that, and you may not be quite so disappointed when it happens. You'll know it's normal. It will confirm that you're still on the writer's path.

Appendix II

The Questionnaire

• •

Here are the questions we asked writers, either in person, by E-mail, or on the phone:

1. Do you remember if there was a period of deep restlessness or unhappiness that preceded your commitment to writing? This could be anytime you started a new project or at the very beginning of your writing career.

2. Do you recall realizing you would have to sacrifice something in order to write?

3. What does it feel like to you when you don't want any distraction, when all you want—or need—to do is work?

4. Please tell us about a moment when a writing dream came true.

5. In regard to your writing, what does the word *commitment* mean to you? Can you tell us a story about it?

6. Would you tell us a story about a time when you were really scared or full of self-doubt about your writing or your writing career?

7. Do you remember wanting to write or wanting to be published? How much did you want it? What was it like for you wanting it that much?

8. When you're working on a book, what's the hardest part?
9. How does it feel when everything's flowing?
10. When are you most likely to fall prey to self-doubt?
11. When it's time to get to work, where would we find you?
12. If you could give only one bit of advice to readers, what would it be?

Sources

· ·

Sources are arranged by order of the appearance of the quotations within each chapter.

The Trailhead

Paul Zalis, *Who Is the River: Getting Lost and Found in the Amazon and Other Places* (New York: Atheneum, 1986).

John Wesley Powell, *Down the Colorado* (New York: Arrowood Press, 1988).

Unhappiness

Walker Percy, quoted in *The Writer's Chapbook*, edited from *The Paris Review Interviews* (New York: Modern Library, 1999).

William Faulkner, quoted in *Writer's Chapbook*.

Eva McCall, from an interview.

Carl G. Jung, quoted in Raymond Corsini, ed., *Current Psychotherapies* (Itasca, Ill.: F. E. Peacock Publishers, 1973).

Jonathan Franzen, quoted in *New York Times*, "Jonathan Franzen's Big Book," Sept. 2, 2001.

Jack Finney, *Time and Again* (New York: Simon and Schuster, 1970).

Annie Proulx, *The Shipping News* (New York: Simon and Schuster, 1994).

J. K. Rowling, *Harry Potter and the Goblet of Fire* (New York: Scholastic Trade, 2002).

Yamamoto Tsunetomo, *The Hagakure* (Tokyo: Kodansha International, 1979).

Oscar Wilde, quoted in *Writer's Chapbook*.

Annette Curtis Klause, *Blood and Chocolate* (Minneapolis, Minn.: Econo-Clad Books, 1999).

Wanting

Émile Zola, quoted in *The Writer's Chapbook*, edited from *The Paris Review Interviews* (New York: Modern Library, 1999).

Bob Dylan, quoted in Peter McWilliams, *The Portable DO IT!* (Los Angeles: Prelude Press, 1995).

Stephen King, *On Writing* (New York: Pocket Books, 2000).

Sterling Hayden, *Wanderer* (Dobbs Ferry, N.Y.: Sheridan House, 1998).

F. Scott Fitzgerald, *The Great Gatsby* (New York: Scribner, 1996).

J. G. Ballard, quoted in *Writer's Chapbook*.

Thomas Mann, quoted in *Writer's Chapbook*.

Books by Robert B. Parker, Barbara Kingsolver, Colin Fletcher, Dennis Lehane, Martha Grimes, Louise Erdrich, Alice Hoffman, Susan Isaacs, Lia Matera, J. K. Rowling, Agatha Christie, James M. Cain, John D. MacDonald, Ngaio Marsh, and Margaret Millar.

T. Jefferson Parker, quoted in Shelly Nix-Schmaltz, *San Diego Chapter of Sisters in Crime News* 11, no. 7 (2001).

Commitment

Dick Bass and Frank Wells with Rick Ridgeway, *Seven Summits* (New York: Warner Books, 1988).

John Wesley Powell, *Down the Colorado* (New York: Arrowood Press, 1988).

Jack London, *The Cruise of the Snark* (Mineola, N.Y.: Dover Publications, 2000).

Lawrence Durrell, quoted in *The Writer's Chapbook*, edited from *The Paris Review Interviews* (New York: Modern Library, 1999).

James Thurber, quoted in *Writer's Chapbook*.

Wavering

Cartoon caption from *Private Eye*, quoted in *The Writer's Chapbook*, edited from *The Paris Review Interviews* (New York: Modern Library, 1999).

Anne Lamott, *Bird by Bird* (New York: Anchor, 1995).

Michael Bane, *Over the Edge: A Regular Guy's Odyssey in Extreme Sports* (Berkeley, Calif.: Wilderness Press, 2000).

Richard Craze, *I Ching* (New York: Sterling Publishing, 2000).

Charles Schulz, *Peanuts* cartoon (date unknown; cut out and found in file).

Antoine de Saint-Exupéry, *The Little Prince* (San Diego, Calif.: Harcourt, 2000).

Christopher Vogler, *The Writer's Journey: Mythic Structure for Writers* (Studio City, Calif.: Michael Wiese Productions, 1998).

E. B. White, quoted in *Writer's Chapbook*.

Gabriele Rico, *Writing the Natural Way* (New York: J. P. Tarcher, 2000).

Lawrence Block, *Writing the Novel: From Plot to Print* (Cincinnati, Ohio: Writer's Digest Books, 1985).

Letting Go

Nikos Kazantzakis, quoted in Peter McWilliams, *The Portable DO IT!* (Los Angeles: Prelude Press, 1995).

John Wesley Powell, *Down the Colorado* (New York: Arrowood Press, 1988).

Lynn Lott, Riki Intner, and Barbara Mendenhall, *Do It Yourself Therapy: How to Think, Feel, and Act Like a New Person in Just 8 Weeks* (Franklin Lakes, N.J.: Career Press, 2000).

Michael Murphy, *In the Zone* (New York: Penguin, 1995).

Immersion

Jack London, *Martin Eden* (New York: Penguin, 1993).

Toni Morrison, quoted in *The Writer's Chapbook*, edited from *The Paris Review Interviews* (New York: Modern Library, 1999).

Gore Vidal, quoted in *Writer's Chapbook*.

Elizabeth Hardwick, quoted in *Writer's Chapbook*.

E. B. White, quoted in *Writer's Chapbook*.

Stephen King, *On Writing* (New York: Pocket Books, 2000).

Lawrence Block, *Writing the Novel: From Plot to Print* (Cincinnati, Ohio: Writer's Digest Books, 1985).

Grace Paley, quoted in *Writer's Chapbook*.

Tony Geiss, *The Random House Dictionary of the English Language* (New York: Random House Trade, 1966).

Anton Chekhov, quoted in *Writer's Chapbook*.

Irwin Shaw, quoted in *Writer's Chapbook*.

Christopher Vogler, *The Writer's Journey: Mythic Structure for Writers* (Studio City, Calif.: Michael Wiese Productions, 1998).

Block, *Writing the Novel*.

Anne Lamott, *Bird by Bird* (New York: Anchor, 1995).

Fulfillment

Thomas Edison, quoted in Peter McWilliams, *The Portable DO IT!* (Los Angeles: Prelude Press, 1995).

Letter from Karl Marx's publisher, quoted in *The Writer's Chapbook*, edited from *The Paris Review Interviews* (New York: Modern Library, 1999).

Marge Piercy, "For the Young Who Want To," *The Moon Is Always Female* (New York: Alfred A. Knopf, 1980, Middlemarsh, Inc.).

Gene Fowler, quoted in *Writer's Chapbook*.

E. L. Doctorow, quoted in *Writer's Chapbook*.

Marianne Moore, quoted in *Writer's Chapbook*.

John Steinbeck, quoted in *Writer's Chapbook*.

John Wesley Powell, *Down the Colorado* (New York: Arrowood Press, 1988).

Other Quotes

The Most Brilliant Thoughts of All Time (In Two Lines or Less), ed. John M. Shanahan (New York: Cliff Street Books, 1999).

Reader's Digest Quotable Quotes (Pleasantville, N.Y.: Reader's Digest, 1997).

The Women's Book of Positive Quotations, compiled and arranged by Leslie Ann Gibson (Minneapolis, Minn.: Fairview Press, 2002).

Acknowledgments
And the Award Goes To . . .

• •

We had a lot of help in the development of this book. We wouldn't have met had it not been for the San Diego chapter of Sisters in Crime, which put together the Bare Bones Writers Conference in Julian, California. Since we live fifteen hundred miles apart, we would have had a tough time writing together without the hospitality of Arlene and Gary Biemiller, Don and Diane Johnson, and Elaine Viets, who graciously shared their places in Florida, all of which overlook water and inspire oodles of creativity. Then there were Jacqui and Bill Bradley, who made sure that there was time for fun as well as work, as they ferried the two authors around the canals of Fort Lauderdale. And then there's Hal Penny, Lynn's husband, who makes her life easier all of the time, and both of our lives easier whenever he's around when we are working. Thank you, Hal, for the morning coffee, the newspapers, the schlepping, the photocopies, and for tiptoeing at just the right times.

Putting together the list of authors to interview was made much easier because of Rebecca Brown, of RebeccasReads.com, who shared names and E-mail addresses of authors who would make likely candidates. Lynn's brother Rick Naymark, president of the Minnesota Public Relations society and member of the board of directors of The

Loft Literary Center, was instrumental in setting up key author interviews, as was Rosemary Blaney, branch manager of Western International Securities, who introduced Lynn to Tom Dorsey.

Before we came up with the list of authors to interview, Lynn asked some friends to fill out the interview form for a trial run. Many thanks to Roy and Janice Beaman, Elisa Baker, Neil Alan, Joan Woodard, Rick Marks, and Lynn's husband, Hal, for taking time to troubleshoot the first interview form. Gratitude to Lynn's clients who have willingly field-tested many of the ideas in this book.

There were many authors who inspired us through their published interviews or speeches, including Jonathan Franzen, T. Jefferson Parker, Elizabeth George, P. D. James, S. J. Hinton, Elizabeth Forsyth Hailey, Donald Riggs, Linda Barnes, Gladys Swan, Mildred Wirt Benson, Susan Elizabeth Phillips, Scott Turow, Barbara Kingsolver, David Baldacci, Yogi Berra, David Kaplan, Sue Grafton, and Steve Cunningham.

Seven autobiographical books urged us on by the sheer drama of their recounting the authors' experiences traveling a path. Two of the books were written by Jack London, and the rest, by John Wesley Powell, Stephen King, Colin Fletcher, Larry McMurtry, and Edward Abbey.

Associations with the work of Virginia Rich, Agatha Christie, Michael Murphy, and Barbara Comfort deepened our understanding of the path, as did books by Anne Lamott, John Gardner, Lawrence Block, Dick Francis, Gabriele Rico, Al Zuckerman, Sheree Bykofsky, Jennifer Basye Sander, Robert B. Parker, Robert McKee, Natalie Goldberg, Julia Cameron, Henriette Anne Klauser, Dorothy Parker, and T. S. Eliot.

We referred often to the *I Ching*, especially the version by Richard Craze, and the UniSun version of *Chinese Fortune Dice*. Nancy's favorite *I Ching* book, *The Complete I Ching*, by the Taoist master Alfred Huang, was a continual source of comfort, inspiration, and enlightenment to her. Those books helped us get unstuck and inspired endless conversations and E-mails about writing. We laughed at many of the quotes in Peter McWilliams's book *The Portable DO IT!* and consulted Lynn's new gift set, written with Rick Naymark and Jane Nelsen, called *Madame Dora's Fortune Telling Cards* (Fairwinds Press) for needed insights. We were challenged by our agents, Janet Rosen (of Sheree Bykofsky Agency) and Meredith Bernstein, to write a book that would reach as many writers as possible.

Artist Paula Gray played an important role in the development of the book when she insisted on a vision of one of the steps that expanded our understanding of it. Later, she produced a map of the steps, using her whimsical drawings and sense of humor, to which we have referred often to help us find our way when we were lost.

Our editor, Linda Marrow, believed in the ideas and encouraged us to write in a manner that spoke clearly to writers at every level.

One lucky night while roaming through bookstores in San Francisco, Lynn came upon a clerk who introduced her to back copies of *The Paris Review*. The clerk remains unnamed, but without his suggestion, many of the quotes in this book would have been missed. Lynn devoured *The Writer's Chapbook*, along with *Beat Writers at Work* and *Women Writers at Work*, and reveled along with Nancy at the wisdom of writers long gone but still with us in spirit.

Nancy spent one lucky weekend as a presenter at the

"Write It, Sell It" Writers Retreat Workshop, founded by the late Gary Provost and run by Gail Provost Stockwell and Lance Stockwell. Everybody there inspired her.

Where Would We Be Without All Those Interviews?

Between us, we interviewed or talked to more than fifty authors. Some of their names appear in the text, whereas others remain unnamed, but all of them have influenced and aided our journey in the writing of this book. If we inadvertently left anyone out, it is from our own carelessness in filing and not because of anything the authors said. Without their help, this book simply would not exist in its current form. We extend our gratitude to the authors for their time, wisdom, and inspiration. Here's the alphabetical list of their names: Rachael Anderson, Shirley Barobs, Barbara Bartocci, Rebecca Brown, Wendy Burt, Eric Burton, Sheree Bykofsky, Jose Climent, Don Coldsmith, Steve Dixon, Tom Dorsey, Roslyn Duffy, Sue Dunlap, Dan Eckstein, Cheryl Erwin, Julie Garwood, Sally Goldenbaum, Judy Goldman, Lori Gotlieb, Sue Grafton, Linda Grant (aka Linda Williams), Tina Hacker, Vinnie Hansen, Norm Harris, Miyoko Hensley, Riki Intner, Richard Keith, Richard Kopp, Martha Lawrence, Gary Legwold, John Lescroart, Rob Mac-Gregor, Trish MacGregor (aka T. J. MacGregor), Jeffrey Marks, Margaret Maron, Lia Matera, Eva McCall, Gary McKay, Barbara Mendenhall, Teresa Miller, Cecil Murphey, Rick Naymark, Jane Nelsen, Kris Neri, Nina Osier, Bobbie J. A. Pfeifer, Martha Powers, Gillian Roberts (aka Judith Greber), Nora Roberts, Kevin Robinson, Lee Schnebly, Lisa Scottoline, Barbara Seranella, Deborah

Shouse, Barbara Unell, Marilyn Wallace, Andrea Warren, Susan White, Earl Williams, and Irene Zabytko.

Most of all, love and thanks to our children, who are walking their own good paths.

About the Authors

Janet Bankovich

LYNN LOTT is a licensed family therapist who holds two master's degrees in counseling and psychology. She has taught parenting, trained family therapists, and worked for years as an associate professor at Sonoma State University. She is a diplomate in the North American Society of Adlerian Psychology, the highest honor of achievement in that group. Her self-help books include *Positive Discipline A–Z*, *Positive Discipline for Teenagers*, *Positive Discipline for Parenting in Recovery*, *Positive Discipline in the Classroom*, *Do-It-Yourself Therapy*, and *Chores Without Wars*. She is the mother of two and stepmother of two, living with her husband and dogs. They divide their time between California and Florida.

NANCY PICKARD has authored sixteen critically acclaimed mystery novels and dozens of short stories. Her popular works have garnered an Anthony Award, a Shamus Award, Agatha Awards, Macavity Awards, and an Edgar nomination. A former president and founding member of Sisters in Crime, she has been a full-time professional writer for thirty-five years. Prior to writing fiction, she worked as a newspaper reporter and editor, a corporate writer, and a freelance writer. She lives in Prairie Village, Kansas.